Hammer It Home

The Complete Guide to Framing Your Dream House

LARRY SOBON &
JACK HAUN

Table of Contents

Book Introduction:

Hey there, builders and DIYers! Are you ready to pick up a hammer and start framing? Whether you're constructing your forever home or just sprucing up the guest house, proper framing is the difference between a sturdy structure and a creaky catastrophe. Grab your tool belt and let's get to it!

Framing is the bones and muscles that hold a house up. It's the skeleton that all the other parts build on. I know what you're thinking, "Framing sounds complicated! All those complex diagrams and architectural specs make my head spin." Well, don't stress, my framing friend! This book breaks down the entire process into simple, step-by-step instructions. We'll go from surveying your foundation to installing the final fascia board. No tricky trigonometry is required! By the time you finish this handy guide, you'll be able to frame a first-class home, from the ground up. We'll cover all the framing fundamentals, like laying a solid sill plate and assembling sturdy stud walls. You'll learn insider tips for framing angled roofs, hanging doors perfectly plumb, and crafting built-in shelving the professional way. Whether your taste runs toward cozy cabins or sleek modern spaces, the right framing techniques will get you there.

For those really ambitious projects, we'll delve into advanced topics like arched doorways, multi-level roofs, and luxurious circular staircases. Picture the satisfied smile on your face as you top off that new gabled addition or stand back and admire your handcrafted portico. Now that's rewarding! This glossy guide has something for framers of every skill level. Newbies can start off simple with a basic backyard shed or garage. Weekend warriors will discover tricks for framing a seamless addition. Experienced house-builders will find in-depth advice for tackling whole houses with flair. Each chapter focuses on a key framing task, with step-by-step instructions, and helpful diagrams to guide you through the process. You'll get insider tips for avoiding common mistakes and troubleshooting any framing flubs along the way.

Whether you're working alone or wrangling a DIY crew, this framing guide has got you covered. We'll walk through coordinating subcontractors, getting proper permits, and staying on schedule for smooth construction. You'll learn smart strategies for saving time and money, without cutting corners, when it comes to safety and structural integrity. Let's plan for the optimally efficient build so you can start enjoying your new space ASAP! With the help of this book, you'll finally understand terms, like a cripple stud, rough sill, and double top plate. Your days of being baffled by building blueprints are over! We'll demystify all those bewildering framing fundamentals until you're talking shear walls and joist hangers like a pro. Soon your custom home will be the talk of the neighbourhood, and you'll proudly give tours, showcasing quality framing from stem to stern.

Whether you're embarking on a serious construction project or just spiffing up your starter home, get ready to frame like an expert craftsman. With a little know-how and a lot of patience, you can build the house of your dreams. Let's get to it! Grab your work gloves, flex those muscles, and let's start framing. This comprehensive guide will arm you with the skills and confidence to create a structurally sound masterpiece. Now go get those saw horses, we've got some ambitious building to do!

Why is proper framing so crucial, anyway, you ask? Well, the framework of your house is like the human skeleton. It shoulders the entire structural load, from gravity pushing down to wind and earthquakes shaking things up! Just like you wouldn't try to hold up a building with jello bones, you need solid framing to support a house long-term. The framework must be precisely aligned, with connections securely fastened to transfer force properly. One weak spot in the framing, and your home's stuck with chronic issues like cracks in drywall or sticking doors. Shoddy framing can even lead to catastrophic failure if a hurricane or earthquake hits! But with care and attention to detail, good framing prevents problems for generations to come. That's where this guide comes in. We'll start by preparing the construction site, getting permits in order, and laying out our floor plan. Location is everything, so we'll carefully site your foundation where it works with the landscape.

Next up, is building a sturdy foundation and concrete slab to tie the whole structure together. We'll frame the floors first, since everything else stacks on top. Joists need to be spaced at precise intervals, so we'll measure meticulously. The subfloor goes down before we stand up the stud walls and shear panels, one by one. Check out those plumb verticals and straight horizontal lines - aesthetics matter too! Once the shell is enclosed, we'll ready the roof for weather proofing. You'll learn how to calculate the ideal roof slope and choose durable, attractive shingles. The roof frame has to hold up under heavy snow, so we'll build in plenty of structural support. You'll find tips for framing bay windows, dormers, and other special features that add character. With strategic framing, you can open up spaces and let light flow in.

Now the fun part - interior finishes! We'll add partition walls to divide rooms. Next, we'll demo cutting door openings and framing arched headers - it's easier than it looks. We'll frame custom cabinetry, shelving, and closet organizers. Oh, and stairs - wait until you see the graceful staircase taking shape. Each meticulously measured and angled stringer, contributes to an elegant floating flow. If walls could talk, these sturdy framing members would have endless stories to tell. They'd reminisce about the satisfying sweat and sawdust of construction, day after day. With so much time and care poured into each board and beam, your home will stand solid for decades to come.

Of course, no framework functions alone. We've got to integrate insulation, HVAC, plumbing, and electrical systems into our framing plan. Building codes and structural calculations will inform each step, but the framing itself is an art. The guidance you'll find here, combined with your vision and labor, will enable you to create a custom dwelling you will be proud to call home. Whether you're embarking on a cabin retreat or building out a stylish loft downtown, framing is the critical first step. Do it right, and your home will provide comfort, craftsmanship, and character for generations to appreciate. Commit to mastering these indispensable skills, and the world's your oyster. Raise a skyscraper, construct a chalet, or frame a tiny house - with solid framing fundamentals, you can build it all.

So what do you say, are you ready to get framing? Grab your tools and let's start constructing! This guide will be here to help you all the way through, from driving the first stake to topping off the roof ridge beam. We have ambitious building to do, but chapter by chapter, you'll gain confidence to tackle any project. Now let's get to work - your dream house awaits!

Chapter 1

Laying the Foundation - Footings, Stem Walls, and More

Welcome to Chapter 1! Before we can actually start framing the floors, walls, and roof of your new home, we need to lay a solid foundation. They say the foundation is the most important part of any structure, and framing is no exception. In this chapter, we'll go over key steps for preparing your building site, digging proper footings, building sturdy foundation walls, and getting ready to frame, right on top.

A friend of mine once told me, "When I built my first house, I was eager to start nailing those floors and stud walls together. But my contractor grabbed me by the shoulders, looked me in the eye, and said, "Kid, you can't build anything worth a darn, without the proper base." At the time, he shrugged him off and figured a quick splash of concrete would do the trick. Well, let's just say that house ended up more crooked than a country fence row! He had to go back and completely re-pour the foundation to salvage the project. Consider that lesson learned. Now we know - the time and care you put into foundation prep and construction, will pay dividends for decades to come.

The right foundation keeps your home sturdy through seasons of expansion and contraction. It resists cracking under the stresses of settling soil, and a level base allows the rest of the framing to stand plumb and true. So don't rush through this part; having patience and precision now, will prevent huge headaches later. In this chapter, we'll methodically walk through each phase of foundation construction together, so you understand the "why" behind every step. We'll start by surveying and preparing your lot by removing vegetation and debris. Next, we'll dig a series of trenches to make way for footing forms. I'll share pointers for laying out perfect corners and calculating trench dimensions from your floor plan. We'll level, square, and brace the footing forms to ensure straight foundation walls.

Mixing and pouring high-strength concrete comes next. I'll help you calculate exactly how many yards of concrete you need for your footings and foundation walls. We'll work together to order materials, organize delivery logistics, and schedule subcontractors. When pouring day arrives, I'll give step-by-step guidance to place concrete, efficiently, without cold joints. Leveling anchor bolts, while the concrete is wet, is crucial for connecting the wood framing later. We'll carefully measure bolt spacing, to match the sill plate. Before the concrete fully cures, we'll backfill the trenches and grade around the foundation. I'll demo various waterproofing techniques to prevent leaks and moisture issues down the road. If you're building on a slope, that will require an extra-beefy, stepped foundation tailored to the terrain. We'll design proper support footings and reinforce the stem walls appropriately. For flood zones and other areas with poor soil, we'll take extra precautions, like pilings or an elevated foundation. The right approach depends on your specific site conditions and local building codes.

By the time we reach the end of this chapter, you'll be able to lay out and dig footing trenches with ease. Forming, framing, pouring, and finishing concrete foundation walls, will feel like second nature. You'll know how to backfill, properly, without compromising structural integrity. Leave the handwriting and sleepless nights to other home builders - your foundation will give you confidence that the rest of the project can stand on it, with zero issues down the road. Now buckle up your tool belt - it's time to start prepping your lot! The very first step is surveying the site and marking the corners with stakes. We'll break out the transit, builder's level, or laser level, and get to work.

When starting construction on any lot, you've got to survey and mark the boundaries first. Property lines legally define the space you have to work with when siting your foundation. Nothing would slow down a project faster than pouring footings where they don't belong! I've seen neighbors come to blows over a few inches of encroachment, so let's avoid that drama by surveying meticulously. You likely received a land survey when you purchased the property, showing corners and boundaries. But it never hurts to do your own verification, just to be 110% sure. Round up a few helpers, grab some tall stakes and colorful tape, and head out to each corner pin. Use a tripod-mounted builder's level, transit, or laser level to align the stakes along the boundary lines. Check angles with the transit, and connect the dots by stretching the mason's string between the stakes.

Make sure property lines have several feet of clearance from any existing structures nearby. Account for overhangs extending past the foundation, when planning the staked corners. If trees or obstacles are in the way, triangulate using multiple sight lines, until all corners are marked clearly. Having accurate corner stakes prevents disputes and keeps the project on track. Once the boundaries are staked out, we can start laying things out!

Now comes the fun part – planning exactly where your new home will sit on the lot! This involves considering setback requirements, views, sunlight exposure, trees, and topography. Local zoning laws dictate minimum front, side, and rear setbacks from the property lines. We'll pull permits to confirm the setback rules for your area before finalizing the floor plan. Hard to enjoy that new great room if it violates the code and has to be torn down! Think about how you want to approach the house when driving up. Curving roads and footpaths create welcoming curb appeal. Account for mature landscaping size when deciding on where you'll place things. Also, take note of prevailing winds, so your deck doesn't end up on the windy side! Mark a few options with stakes and use the site as if you lived there already. Stroll around and envision daily routines like unloading groceries or walking the dog. The house position that "feels right" probably is.

Once you've selected a good spot, we'll tie perpendicular strings and add stakes to mark all four corners of the foundation. Leave some extra space between the strings and pins for the trenches we'll dig soon. Use temporary paint or chalk lines to sketch the outline of the whole house on the ground. This makes it easy for everyone to visualize the final layout. Adjust and re-tweak the position until you have a floor plan you're excited about. Once you're happy with the location of the house, you can shift your focus to preparing the site. This involves clearing vegetation, removing topsoil, re-grading, and excavating where needed. We'll likely need permits for earthwork, stormwater management, and disposal of cleared materials offsite. It's smart to start the permit process early so you're ready to hit the ground running!

Any grass, roots, and organic matter need to go before the digging begins. Plants release moisture and gases that cause foundation cracking and settling, so remove shrubs, sod, and stumps which may be growing near the foundation zone. An experienced excavation subcontractor can make quick work of vegetation removal using bulldozers, backhoes, skid-steers, and bucket loaders. Clear several feet of brush, surrounding the outline of the foundation, so there will be ample room to work.

Next, we'll strip off the topsoil, exposing the firmer subsoil underneath. Topsoil contains lots of organic matter, which compresses, too much, for a stable base. Haul this offsite for reuse elsewhere, or sell it to landscapers. Excavators make this step fast by "peeling" off layers with toothed buckets. Remove topsoil at least a foot beyond the foundation perimeter. With the lot cleared down to mineral soil, it's grading time! We need to create a smooth, gently sloped pad that sheds water and directs it away from the foundation. Sandy, loamy soils drain well if graded at 2-3% slope. Dense clays may need 4-5% or more. Steeper slopes can lead to erosion and foundation destabilization. Get a concept grading plan from your architect to guide this important step.

Speaking of water, a damp lot can wreak havoc on foundations, warping the wood framing and leaching inside. For wet, low-lying areas, install drain pipes, around the perimeter footer, to intercept groundwater before it enters. Or, bring in loads of gravel to build up the lot above the water table. Just pray you don't hit solid rock when excavating! We may need jackhammers, dynamite or foundation piers to solve that headache.

Once the lot is cleared, graded, and drained properly, we're finally ready to start digging our footing trenches! This is a big milestone. Looking at the freshly scraped dirt and boundary lines, the home's footprint will start to feel real now. Next, we'll form the trenches, pour footings, and finally build the stem walls. But first things first - it's time to break ground! We recommend renting a mini excavator for digging footing trenches, unless your site is huge. They're easy to operate with instructions, versatile, and give you better control than huge backhoes. Plus, it's satisfying to shape the trenches yourself! Just be sure to call in underground utility locations so you don't hit any gas pipes or power lines by accident. That would seriously rain on our foundation parade.

Plan where you'll temporarily store the excavated soil and have wheelbarrows ready. Digging will go faster with an eager helper hauling dirt while you operate the excavator. Start by trenching along the outer perimeter of the house first. Twelve to 24 inches wide, is standard, for single-family homes, with a minimum 12-inch depth. It's a bit wider for deeper basements. Safety step-downs may be required around the inside.

Inside corners usually need an extra square footing. Check your blueprints! Avoid sharp 90-degree trenches, which can crack under stress. Go for 45-degree cripple studs, instead. Mark corner points with stakes, then use Mason's string lines on stakes to outline the trenches. Measure from the string to check the width and depth as you dig. Get those lines nice and taut - tight string equals straight trenches. Don't rush the process, or your foundation will pay the price later. For concrete edge forms, metal is stronger, but wood forms like 2x10s work, too. We'll assemble them into boxes, with vertical stakes to brace, in the next step. Footing width depends on load; for a single-story home, 16 inches wide is common if the soil quality is decent. A deeper frost line equals wider footings. Soil tests tell us how wide and deep we need to go in your area.

Alright, we've got crisp, perfectly square trenches fully excavated! Now comes a VERY important step - trench inspection. I've learned the hard way; nothing is worse than pouring concrete, only to realize the trenches got mismeasured. Call to schedule an official inspection and don't proceed until you pass. The building official will check the width, depth, slope, and level and look for improper material in the trenches. With the green light from inspection, we're cleared to start assembling the form. Trench walls may need bracing so they don't slough off. Use wood or metal forms, secured with stakes, driven at least 1 foot outside the trench. Metal forms are sturdy, while wood forms, like 2x10 lumber, accept nails better, and remember tonstall 'whalers' across the top to reinforce the form walls.

Carefully measure inside dimensions between the forms as you assemble - accuracy matters big time! The tops of the forms must be perfectly level, which we'll check with a line level or laser level. Consistent depth is critical, so the foundation sits on stable, uniform soil across the entire footprint. Don't forget interior footings under posts or bearing walls!

Next, we'll establish the elevation of the top of the footing. The concrete will need to reach the top of the footing. Use a transit on a tripod, or laser level, to mark the height on stakes driven behind the forms. The elevation accounts for the footer depth, stem wall height, and desired frame wall height. Double and triple-check the numbers here - mistakes are not easy to fix later!

With the form work complete, inspected, and ready for concrete, let's move on to preparing for the big pour! First, we'll call a concrete company and order the amount we need. Footing concrete uses higher strength mixes, like 3000 PSI. With the total linear footage of your footings, we can calculate the exact quantity. Leave a little extra so you don't run short. Scheduling the truck delivery is critical, since concrete starts curing immediately after it's mixed. With a few friends for help, we can move 5+ yards an hour. Have wheelbarrows, concrete rakes, and floats ready to go. The inspector will need to approve the pour and check that we don't have cold joints between batches. You'll love watching the mud transform into a smooth, sturdy foundation! Next, bolt the wood sill plate to the foundation, securing the rest of the framing. Using a template with proper spacing, hammer in the bolts so they protrude to the right height above the finished concrete. They need to be centered on the footing, parallel, and spaced evenly. Anchor bolt specs depend on your design; the hardware store has everything we need.

Lastly, plan where concrete trucks will pump it in. Clear access paths and make sure pumps can reach every footing trench. Have helpers ready with shovels and wheelbarrows to transport concrete quickly. We'll work as a team to pour efficiently. Don't forget to use re-bar, if specified, for reinforcement!. Get ready for an intense but satisfying day!

Alright, foundation tour! Let's walk through a properly poured concrete footing and foundation wall assembly. After digging the trenches and building forms, that re-bar mat gets lowered in for reinforcing. Then carefully measured concrete fills the trench, smoothing with a screed as we pour. Don't forget the anchor bolts!

Next, we'll erect the stem wall forms on top of the cured footing. These hold the concrete for shorter foundation walls, or full basement walls if it's an excavated basement. Make sure wall forms are braced plumb, and corners precisely 90 degrees. Reinforcing here too, either rebar or fiber mesh, depending on local codes and seismic factors. Pouring the stem walls is similar to footings. You'll need wheelbarrows, and there will be pumping and screeding. Leave openings for big windows and doors if needed. Once cured, we'll backfill, with a gravel base, then topsoil. Strip forms when the concrete reaches 1500 PSI strength. Then we install foundation waterproofing, protection board, and below-grade drainage. These steps are essential for dry, stable basements!

Congratulations, your footing and foundation walls are complete!. Now your house has sturdy "bones" to build upon. Pat yourself on the back, you've earned it. Next, we'll start framing floors and assembling those walls. The fun with wood starts soon! But for now, let's appreciate all the hard work so far. Stop and visualize your rooms sitting on this solid base. It's going to be beautiful. Now, we've got some serious framing coming right up!

Now that the concrete has cured, we've got a solid foundation ready for framing floors and walls. But first, a critical step - installing the mudsill, aka the sill plate. This is a treated wood board that sits atop the foundation and anchors the rest of the structure. Let's focus today on best practices for sill plate installation. The ideal material is pressure-treated lumber, which resists moisture and rotting. 2x6 or 2x8 dimensions are common. Use lumber that's straight, knot-free, and warp-free to ensure even contact with the foundation. Match the mudsill width to the thickness of your framed walls.

Prep the foundation surface so it's flat and smooth. Chip away any loose material or honeycombs. Grind down bumps or ridges in the concrete. Fill divots with a non-shrinking cement-like hydraulic concrete mix. The sill plate must mate tightly to the foundation along its entire length. Now we can start placing the mudsill. If there's a joint, stagger pieces so they don't meet over openings, like doors. Anchor tightly using the bolts we set in the concrete earlier. Tighten washers and nuts securely, but not so much that they crack the sill plate. Consistent anchoring is crucial! Inspect the mudsill alignment, obsessively, as you set it. Use a level, often, to ensure it's completely straight and flat across the entire foundation. Tap shims under low spots to stabilize. We want full contact, everywhere, for proper load transfer. Don't proceed until the sill plate sits perfectly level all the way around.

For foundations with steps and elevation changes, use galvanized metal tie straps. These reinforce the joints between sill plate sections of different heights. Changes in height mean changes in load transfer, so we've got to tie them together structurally. Proper reinforcement here prevents cracks later. Optionally, the adhesive can create an even stronger sill plate bond. Construction adhesive caulk works great, but remember to apply in a thick layer before setting the sill plate. But don't skip the anchor bolts! Adhesive, alone, won't reliably hold the plate down. We need the anchors for their focused compressive strength. The adhesive just supplements this grip. If the foundation edges are rough or uneven, consider a foam adhesive to attach the sill plate. This cushions and insulates the sill plate from the concrete. The foam lets the plate mate tightly, to uneven surfaces, by conforming to small gaps and bumps. Just be sure to anchor and fasten adequately through the foam.

For concrete block stem walls, take extra care shimming and anchoring the sill plate. The blocks have more unevenness than the poured walls. Use lots of construction adhesive to seal air gaps, and significantly more anchor bolts. Irregular tension across block foundations can destabilize the framing if we're not extremely diligent here.

Let's talk about wood fungal decay and termites, the natural enemies of any wood-framed structure. The sill plate's direct concrete contact makes it especially vulnerable to moisture, wicking up from below. Water attracts wood-eating insects that chew away unseen until major damage is done. Prevention now, saves huge repairs down the road. Use fungicidal copper naphthenate solution, to pressure-treat exposed sill plate surfaces. This soaks deep into the grain, killing existing fungus and preventing new growth. Re-apply annually for ongoing protection. For stubborn fungal growth, bleach or hydrogen peroxide works well too. Just rinse thoroughly so you don't degrade the concrete. For termite prevention, Boracare powder or borate solution treats the surrounding soil as a barrier. The minerals disrupt the termites' exoskeletons and digestive systems. Apply liberally, under and around the sill, to deter those hungry homewreckers. Physical termite barriers like stainless steel mesh also obstruct access from below.

Let's move up from the foundation now and talk about framing platform floors on the newly installed sill plate. Platform framing is the standard for residential construction; it means building each level as a separate floor "platform," rather than interacting. This makes construction fast and flexible.

The floor joists tie into the sill plate with joist hangers, spaced according to your plans. We'll measure meticulously so they're precisely centered for consistent support. Use twist-proof joist hangers with inside flanges so they can't deflect outward. Nail them securely through the pre-punched side holes.

Run the joist lengthwise with the shortest dimension of the floor plan to reduce sagging. For long joist spans, use engineered joists designed for strength. Check the joist specs to see if solid blocking is needed between them for stabilization. Don't cut corners here! Proper joist layout prevents squeaky floors later on.

Okay, time to talk subflooring! The subfloor goes atop the joists to tie the structure together laterally. Use tongue and groove-oriented strand board (OSB) sheets. Stagger the joints and use construction adhesive and screws to fasten to the joists below. Don't just nail the subfloor - those sheets need robust anchoring to keep the floor bounce in check. Do you have floor openings planned, like stairs or chimneys? Box and frame those openings with headers and trimmer joists for structural continuity. The subfloor needs full perimeter support, so blocking frames around openings keeps the edges stiff. We'll cut out the floor section later after framing the walls.

Watch for fireblocking! We've got to seal up concealed spaces to obstruct fire from spreading from room to room. Fire stops made of wood or caulk plug hidden pathways in floor and ceiling cavities. Don't forget this crucial step! It could save lives down the road. Inspectors will be looking closely for proper fire blocking throughout the framing.

Okay, we've meticulously installed the sill plate, floor joists, and subfloor. Now we're finally ready to start framing some walls! In the next chapter, we'll dive into framing techniques to create straight, plumb stud walls, locked tightly into our completed floor platform. Get some rest - we've got an exciting framing journey ahead!

Chapter 2

Framing Floors - Joists, Subfloors, and Structural Considerations

Let's get down to the business of framing up those floors! A solid foundation deserves an equally sturdy framework built upon it. Floor framing ties the whole structure together, so we've got to get it right. Grab your tape measure, because those floor joists need to line up perfectly on the center. We'll start by plotting out our floor plan and marking where each framing member will go. Planning ahead is crucial - once those foundation walls and concrete floors are poured, we're committed to the layout. It's best to use engineered wood I-joists for the floor framing. They're lightweight but incredibly strong. We'll pick joists deep enough to span our full floor dimensions without sagging. For a 12-foot span, 10-inch I-joists spaced 16 inches on center should do the trick. We'll stagger the joist layout where the upper floors bear down on the ones below.

Laying out the joists is all about precision measuring between the sill plates. We want nice straight joists, so take the time to line them up vertically plumb. The slightest bit of skew, in one joist, multiplies across the whole floor, into a sloping mess! Let's build this baby straight and true. Mark the joist locations on the sill plates with chalk lines before setting the joists in place. We'll place rim boards, with sturdy 10d nails, every 16 inches into the sill plate. I prefer angling in pairs from both sides for maximum gripping power. The glue between the sill plates and joists, adds extra rigidity too. Bridging between the joists mid-span keeps them straight and reduces bounce. We'll cut and fit solid blocking, snugly, between each pair. Leave a tiny gap so they don't push out the joists when nailed in place. Speaking of which, never drive nails near the edges - they'll split the wood! Keep nails centered for strength.

With all our joists lined up perfectly, we're ready to start installing the subfloor. These sheets of sturdy plywood get nailed across the tops of the joists to tie them together, into one solid floor. We'll use 8d, ring shank nails, every 6 inches, around the perimeter and down through the sheet midpoint over each joist. Offset the seams between subfloor sheets, so they don't all line up on the same joists. Ah subfloor, the unsung hero of any good framed floor. It not only braces the joists but also stiffens the entire floor as one rigid diaphragm. That's important for resisting lateral loads that can shear a floor apart. We'll drive nails every 6 inches around the perimeter of each sheet, and then stagger additional nails in a grid across the field. These subfloor sheets are heavy, so get a friend to help lift and fit them into place. We don't want to be riding a sheet down like a magic carpet! Set it gently atop the joists and take care of aligning edges and ends over our layout lines. Then we can roll it out and nail it off before moving on to the next sheet.

Don't be shy with nails on the subfloor; the more the merrier. They cinch everything together and reduce squeaks that drive homeowners crazy. We'll use ring shank nails or even screw down the sheets for maximum grip. Stagger the end seams between rows and leave a tiny 1/8-inch gap for expansion at the perimeter. Installing insulation between the joists is definitely worth the effort, even on upper floors. It pays off exponentially in comfort and energy savings. Just make sure to avoid stuffing the cavities so full that it pushes out on the joists. That defeats the purpose by misaligning everything! Let's lightly fill between joists but leave room for air circulation.

The first key is properly tying floors to the foundation. That connection transfers all vertical and horizontal loads down to the footings, so it's crucial. We'll bolt our wood sill plates to the foundation wall with 1/2-inch anchor bolts, spaced 4 feet apart.g Simpson Strong Tie hold downs can be used for extra cinching power at wall corners. Speaking of which, corners need special attention when framing floors. We have to carry loads from both directions, so let's beef things up with extra blocking between the joists. While we're at it, any wall openings will get doubled-up headers and tightly spaced cripple studs to maintain rigidity.

Now we get to frame those bay windows, cantilever overhangs, and other special features that add character. But remember - aesthetics never compromise structural integrity! Let me walk you through how to frame curves and angles while maintaining strength.

Bay windows jut out to expand the view, but they create gaps that weaken the floor framing. We'll frame a reinforced stub wall underneath to pick up the load. Make sure to extend joists full length under the bay; never notch or hang them short. Glue and nails tie this stub framing back to the main structure. Cantilevers projecting past the exterior wall pose a similar dilemma. But with a few tricks, we can achieve that floating appearance and keep it robust. The key is beefing up joists under the cantilever, with doubled 2x material. We'll anchor them at interior walls and wrap them in plywood gussets for maximum stiffness. Cathedral ceilings open up interior spaces but require special framing adaptations. Typically, we'll install raised top plates on stud walls to extend higher. Make sure these raised plates are anchored together at the center! Then we can frame roof rafters right to the taller walls for dramatic sloped ceilings.

Next, let's take a minute to talk about best practices for notching and boring holes in joists. I know - not the most glamorous topic. But, improper cuts are the #1 cause of failed framing inspections! So, pay attention and let's do this by the book. Notches in the top or bottom of the joist cannot exceed 1/6 the depth. That leaves plenty of intact wood to carry loads. Holes bored should be centered and no wider than 1/3 the joist depth. Remember to keep all cuts well away from joint locations, and never notch near supports like beams or posts! To prep for tile, hardwood, or carpet, we recommend screwing down a 1/4 inch backer board before laying finish tiles. We'll install peel-and-stick underlayment over the subfloor if the plan is carpeting or wood flooring. Either way, a nice, smooth, flat surface makes for happy feet.

You're shaping into quite the floor framing pro! Setting sturdy foundations and frameworks is so fulfilling. All those carefully measured joists and interlocking subfloor sheets already feel rock-solid. Just think - generations will walk, play, cook, laugh, and live their lives supported by the floors we framed today. Now that's job satisfaction! The intrinsic rewards from building something worthwhile make all the sweat and soreness worthwhile. Now that we've got the basics of floor framing down, let's go over some advanced techniques for creating unique, custom floors. If you're aiming to build something beyond the ordinary, pay close attention!

Sometimes design visions call for curved walls or circular floor plans. These gracefully rounded shapes require unconventional framing adaptations. Trying to bend solid lumber joists would risk creaking and failure. The solution? Using thin laminated veneer lumber (LVL) or flexible engineered I-joists. LVL is composed of multiple thin wood plies glued together under pressure. That laminated construction allows it to flex and curve without compromising strength. Let's design free-flowing rounded floor plans by framing them with gracefully curved LVL rim boards and joists. The veneer faces resist buckling despite the bends. Or, we can achieve similar flexible results using deep I-joists made with rigid top and bottom flanges but flexible oriented strand board webbing in between. That allows the I-joist to flex and curve without distorting the wood or popping nails. Manufacturers even make circular I-joists for framing perfect domed spaces.

Beyond curving lumber, we also need strategies for attaching subfloor to joists along rounded walls. Hard, rigid sheets of plywood don't bend so easily! For smooth curves, look to interlocking subfloor panels. These are designed with grooved edges that clip together without nails. We can install them in sweeping curves. For tighter radii, backer boards made from thin bending plywood work better than thick subfloor sheets. Let's cut the plywood into narrow horizontal strips. Soak them in water to make the wood pliable, then bend and nail them into place along the curved joists. Use plenty of construction adhesive to keep them adhered.

That covers creating flowing, curvilinear floors. Now let's tackle some unorthodox multilevel designs. Say we're framing a sunken living room, split-level addition, or rooms with dramatic steps and staging. How do we break up floors into distinct levels? The key is staggered platforms built off the main floor, using careful step-downs in joists. We'll frame each platform section independently, and then bridge between them. To step joists down halfway, notch them over a supporting girder beam. We can notch in full steps, or taper incrementally, depending on the desired look. In areas with minimal headroom below, a sturdy ledger secured to the band joist can support step-downs instead of notching joists. We'll nail joist hangers to the stepped ledger, keeping their tops aligned.

Mini-platforms framed between beams build out additional floor levels wherever needed.

No matter how many levels, the floors have to flow together cohesively. Let's mark carefully planned layouts on the foundation before pouring concrete footings. That ensures aligned sidewalls and beams that transition floors smoothly. We'll frame connectors and block between platforms for maximum unity and rigidity.

Truly advanced layouts can be designed, like framed radial floors. Imagine floor joists radiating outward from a central focal point, like spokes on a wheel. This creates unique circular, polygonal, or maze-like floor plans. Framing them takes meticulous planning and patient execution. First, we'll mark an accurate center point and use trammel points to trace the perimeter curves on the foundation. Next, mirror our joist layout in all directions, keeping equal radial spacing. Use tapered blocking adapters where larger radial joists intersect the perimeter bands.

Cut tapered cants to seamlessly bridge odd joist angles. Lay the subfloor in segmented pieces, trimming wedges to follow the concentric contours. Think tangram puzzles - we'll fill the space creatively without leaving gaps. Expect brain-bending challenges, but the gorgeous results are worth it! Alright, your minds must be spinning after all that. Let's take a deep breath and reground ourselves before moving on. These advanced techniques prove, with care and imagination, we can frame floors in any conceivable shape. But now let's get back to essentials that apply to every flooring project imaginable. Namely, how to build a robust, level, and long-lasting floor structure. I promised practical advice, so I'll focus the rest of this chapter on mundane, but crucial, best practices. Apply these guiding principles, and you'll never need to worry about a sagging subfloor or noisy squeaky joists.

The simplest tip? Use quality lumber and properly acclimate it onsite before building. Warped, twisted, or cracked beams and joists undermine structural integrity from the start. Carefully inspect each piece and reject any with major defects before installing. Proper acclimation prevents shrinkage or expansion after framing. Speaking of lumber quality, never scrimp on engineered wood products like LVL beams and I-joists. Shop fabricated in climate-controlled factories, these composites offer reliable strength and straightness. Use hurricane ties and gang nail plates, when joining engineered wood for impeccable connections. Assuming pristine lumber is secured with robust metal ties, bracing is the next key for fail-proof floors. Always brace perimeter joists with solid blocking. Structural panels, like plywood sheathing, add massive rigidity when fastened properly. Adhesives glue it all together permanently.

Let's also spend time shimming and nailing the subfloor, until every seam is flush. Sand down any ridges or hammer down protruding nail heads. We want to start finishing floors with the smoothest, flattest substrate possible. That prevents cracks or divots from telegraphing through. Once all sections are completed, the last step is framing structural connections between new additions and existing buildings. This is critical, yet often neglected. Let's properly tie and support abutting floor structures, so they move and settle in unison over the years. Okay, my friends, we've framed, braced, tied, and fortified one heck of a floor structure! Feel free to walk across this puppy in work boots - it can handle the weight. You all should feel proud looking back at the complex challenges we navigated together in this chapter. Pat yourselves on the back, grab some dinner, and rest up for tomorrow. More adventures in framing await, but we'll build on the sturdy foundation constructed today.

Chapter 3

Framing Walls - Studs, Plates, Headers, and Openings

Framing up walls is the next crucial step after laying the foundation and floor joists. Wall framing consists of vertical studs and horizontal elements, like plates and headers, that tie the structure together. In this chapter, we'll delve into framing basics like determining stud layout, constructing corners and openings, aligning studs properly, and reinforcing with bracing. With the right techniques, you can frame sturdy, attractive walls to enclose your space. We'll cover how to select suitable lumber, use tools, like levels and string lines, to ensure straight walls and follow best practices for assembly. You'll learn tips for laying out studs, plates, and headers based on your floor plan. We'll also discuss advanced framing techniques to maximize energy efficiency.

Let's start at the bottom with our sill plate. This is the horizontal board that sits directly on the foundation, securing the wall studs above. Use pressure-treated lumber for a rot-resistant sill plate that withstands moisture. Anchor it to the foundation with galvanized bolts spaced 16" to 24" apart. Staggering bolts prevent splitting the sill plate. If your foundation has anchor bolts pre-installed, align the sill plate carefully over them. With the sill plate secured, now we can stand up the vertical wall studs. Standard dimensions for wall studs are 2x4 or 2x6 lumber, spaced 16" or 24" apart. Choose the larger 2x6 size if you need room for more insulation. Stud spacing depends on the load-bearing needs of your wall. Heavy upper floors or roofs require 16" spacing for sufficient support. Standard exterior walls and interior partitions can handle 24" stud spacing. Let's lay out our first wall section. Measure and mark the sill plate where each stud will go, keeping them evenly spaced. Angle your tape measure up from each mark to extend layout lines up the entire wall height. Build each wall in sections, no longer than 10 feet, to manage weight and transport before standing them up.

Now we're ready to cut studs to length and assemble the wall section flat on the floor. Start by nailing the end studs to the sill plate with two angled nails. Make sure wall studs are crowned outward, so any bowing under the load pushes them tighter against sheathing later. Continue nailing the remaining studs to the sill plate. Double-check stud spacing, using a level, frequently, to realign them vertically. Temporary X-bracing keeps the wall section square as you work. Finally, nail on a top plate, overlapping corners, and staggering joints. Hoist the finished wall section up into position, plumbed vertically, and braced temporarily, until sheathing and permanent braces are added.

For exterior walls, apply house wrap over the studs before installing siding material. This water-resistant barrier protects from moisture intrusion while allowing walls to breathe. Use flashing to seal around windows, doors, and joints. Careful detailing prevents leaks as you envelop your framed shell.

Now let's frame some wall openings for windows and doors. This involves sizing the header and trimmer studs, to carry the load above and beside the opening. The rule of thumb is to use a header the same width as the wall studs. So, in a 2x4 wall, build a double 2x4 header, and for 2x6 construction, use a double 2x6 header. Span tables provide exact specifications for header sizing based on opening width. Trimmer studs should be at least two-thirds the width of full studs to adequately support the header. Cut jack and king studs above and below the opening to tie into the header and sill. For large openings, like garage doors, engineered headers, or laminated strand, lumber is stronger than typical dimensional lumber. An engineer can specify the ideal product and size for your opening span. Don't forget about trimmer studs, jack studs and cripple studs too. A complete professional framing job results in beautifully plumb and centered openings, every time.

Let's move on to constructing interior walls and partitions. The process is similar, but interior walls are not load-bearing, so they can handle wider stud spacing and slimmer lumber. Stick with 2x4 studs and 24" spacing for most interior applications. For bathrooms and kitchens, use moisture-resistant drywall or cement board instead of standard drywall. Sometimes you'll need to frame odd angles or sweeping curves to meet your aesthetic vision. After laying out the wall path, cut each stud to fit the unique shape. Kerf cuts allow bending lumber to the desired angle. Secure angled studs well to plates and headers, to prevent future sagging. Scribe final trim pieces, later, for a seamless finish.

Wall framing intersections require careful planning, too. Use three-stud corners at outside corners for rigidity. Stagger walls so joints don't align to transfer loads properly. Ensure connection points to land on common studs are secured well with nails or construction adhesive. Adequate bracing is critical to prevent walls from shifting under pressure. Speaking of which, let's discuss wall bracing next. Bracing includes blocks between studs, diagonal wood or metal straps, and structural sheathing to stiffen the frame. Brace exterior walls at a minimum every 25 feet. Bracing requirements vary based on seismic and wind zones, so check your building plans. In hurricane-prone regions, structural panels, like plywood or OSB sheathing over framing, substantially increase resistance to wind pressure. Stagger panel seams and use adhesive and nails spaced 4" to 6" apart around the full perimeter. Metal straps offer adjustable tension strength for wall and roof bracing.

Don't neglect interior wall bracing, either. Include cut-to-fit blocking between studs, especially at heavy fixtures, like cabinets or wall-mounted TVs. The goal is continuous load transfer from the roof to the foundation without weak points that can lead to cracks or collapse. Diagonal bracing resists lateral forces from wind or earthquakes. Rounding corners requires careful framing techniques too. Start by measuring and marking stud positions on both walls at an equal distance from the corner. Cut studs to form mitered corners. Where they overlap, secure stud pairs together with construction adhesive and joist hangers. Minimal metal hardware maximizes corner strength. Alternatively, frame normal square corners with filler studs added in the corner bay. This three-stud corner method avoids weak miter joints. Drywall finishes will hide the filled corner bay. Just take care to stagger adjacent wall studs, so joints don't align at stress points like corners. For arched openings, use laminated veneer lumber, shapeable with kerf cuts or steam bending. Anchor curved studs well, to headers and sill plates. Wider top plates allow adjusting stud spacing to follow the arch layout. You can also frame rectangular openings and scribe drywall later for arched shapes. The framing itself remains plumb and square.

That covers the basics of laying out and assembling stud walls. But we should also discuss advanced framing techniques to boost energy efficiency and material savings. Strategies like two-stud corners, 24" on-center studs, insulated headers, and aligned framing improve performance. With two-stud corners, drywall attaches to a single row of studs with back-blocking where needed. This allows thicker insulation batts between studs without compression gaps. Stick with 24" on-center stud spacing throughout for consistent insulation, and align floors, walls, and roof framing to minimize thermal bridging through wood. Use rigid foam insulation under headers to prevent cold air infiltration above windows and doors. You can purchase pre-made insulated headers, or cut your own insulation inserts to fit. The added R-value blocks convection and improves comfort tremendously.

These advanced framing techniques take a little extra planning up front, but the energy savings and sustainability gains make it worthwhile. The insulation value of your walls has a huge impact on heating and cooling costs and occupant comfort. So, take the time to frame thoughtfully, and it will pay dividends for years to come. Before moving on from wall framing, let's do a quick quality check. Are all your studs plumb and properly aligned? Make sure there are no crown reversals or bowing studs. Are spacings accurate throughout according to the code? Are plates and corners tightly joined? Are openings sized correctly, with adequate headers and jack studs? The details matter here, so inspect each component, as you go, and make any needed adjustments. Use levels, string lines, square tools, and plumb bobs, liberally, to confirm everything is square, level, and structurally sound. Solid walls prevent problems down the road, so repeat checking steps until it's right.

Your stud walls are up, and you've learned tons about structural framing techniques! With practice, these steps will become second nature as you frame houses intuitively. But take your time early on, measure precisely, and don't be afraid to re-do steps for straight, robust framing. You're well on your way to enclosing a comfortable, durable living space. In the next chapter, we'll move up to the roof, discussing various roofing styles and framing considerations. Roof framing requires calculating rafter angles and spans, as we frame the gables and roof deck. I'll share tips for choosing roofing materials and properly insulating attic spaces as well.

But for now, stand back and admire your handiwork on these walls. Feel the satisfaction of learning new skills and building something sturdy with your own hands. You've done quality work, so soak it in before we dive into roofs next. Knowing these wall framing fundamentals will prove invaluable, in every future building project. Now that we've covered wall framing fundamentals, let's go over some best practices for quality and efficiency. Careful planning and precision in layout and cutting will save you time, materials, and headaches down the road.

First, thoroughly read the entire building plan and understand each wall's purpose before framing. Identify load-bearing walls that require 16" o.c. studs and any special structural considerations. Also note interior, non-load-bearing partitions, that can utilize 24" o.c. spacing. Next, organize your lumber deliveries so that needed sizes and lengths are available when the wall is framed. Grouping walls by stud spacing helps streamline the process. Prepare detailed cut lists, noting dimensions and quantities of plates, studs, headers, and other framing members. When laying out, use the 3-4-5 rule to square corners and double check with diagonal measurements. Mark stud locations with chalk lines snapped between points for straight vertical layout lines. Triple-check all major measurements before cutting.

Cut plates and studs with a quality miter or circular saw for fast, clean results. Set the saw depth just shy of the thickness to avoid cutting into fixtures below. Clamp guides to ensure straight cuts. Label pieces and assemble walls flat on the decking whenever possible. Work systematically around the structure, when erecting walls. Complete exterior load-bearing walls first, then interior partitions. Keep walls braced as you go and fasten connections securely. Use pyramid braces, plank strapping, or sheathing, right away, for stability. Plumb each stud individually, as you nail them to stay square. To straighten slightly crooked studs, placewood wedges, into the gap, at connections. Recheck the plumb, often, using a 4' level. Keep seams aligned and gaps under 1/8" for proper load transfer. Inspect all finished walls, thoroughly, before moving on. Are studs straight, plumb, and at proper spacing? Are plates and corners tightly fastened? Are all openings framed correctly? Take photos and detailed notes about any issues to remedy later.

Now we'll review the material selection for wall framing. The most common choices are dimensional lumber, engineered wood, or light gauge steel. Let's compare the pros and cons of each option.

Dimensional lumber, like 2x4 and 2x6 boards, are a familiar go-to. They're readily available at local lumber yards. Pine, fir, and spruce are common wood species used. Just check moisture content before use. Kiln-dried is ideal. Pros of dimensional lumber include its strength, workability, and natural appearance. Cons are variability in straightness and susceptibility to warping or splitting, over time. It must be protected from moisture exposure.

Engineered wood, like LVL or I-joists, are manufactured for structural use with improved consistency and no warping. They resist twisting forces well. LVL also enables long clear spans. Initial material cost is higher than standard lumber, though.

Light gauge steel studs offer exceptional stability, perfect for tall walls or high seismic/wind zones. Steel has high strength and won't shrink or warp. Cons are higher material and labor costs and less insulation capacity than wood studs.

Consider snow, wind, and seismic factors for your region, as well as budget, when selecting framing materials. Qualified suppliers can help specify the ideal products to meet local building codes too. Along with following building codes, safety is a top prioriety, as well. Remember these tips for safety, when framing walls and lifting them into place. Be cautious of falls and wear proper equipment like harnesses and hard hats on sites. Make sure no utilities are routed through an area before framing walls or posts.
Inspect all equipment and lifts routinely. Rig wall sections securely and check balance before lifting. Use tag lines and multiple helpers, to stabilize walls as they are tilted up. Install temporary braces, immediately, after the plumbing walls are vertical.

Stack materials neatly and clear debris, often, to prevent slips or tripping hazards. Wear eye and ear protection when operating power saws, and keep cords organized and tools in good, operating condition. Take breaks to avoid fatigue, the cause of many job site accidents. Work carefully on ladders or scaffolding. Inspect for defects and use proper access equipment. Don't overload or overreach - reposition items nearby, rather than stretching unsafely. Keep your focus and don't rush through challenging tasks.

Lastly, let's discuss techniques for anchoring framed walls securely. This critical step transfers loads down through the structure, into the foundation. Use galvanized metal connectors resistant to rust and wood decay. Anchor walls to floor framing with hurricane ties, which are usually made of galvanized steel. Nail them between studs and joists at a 45-degree angle. They firmly tie walls to floors, along the entire perimeter. Use 2-3 per stud bay, spaced 4 feet apart or less. At foundations, bolt plates to poured walls or slab perimeter stem walls. For raised foundations, bolt sill plates directly to posts or beams. A continuous load path is vital for stability.

In multi-story buildings, use framing connectors between floors and walls. Position joists or truss hangers under parallel walls above. Solid blocking and adhesive creates a sturdy composite unit. Thoroughly brace and anchor all walls, immediately, after framing for safety during construction. Don't move on until every stud, wall, opening, and intersection is secured and stabilized properly.

There you have it - expert techniques to frame walls efficiently with quality results. Follow these tips for satisfying builds. Take pride in learning this fundamental part of homebuilding. With framing know-how, you can erect the bones of any residential or commercial structure. Wall framing skills allow you to translate floorplans into inhabitable spaces that stand the test of time. You're now equipped to build it right the first time!

Chapter 4

Framing Roofs - Rafters, Trusses, and Roof Styles

The roof is one of the most essential parts of a home's framework. It keeps the elements out and provides structural support for the entire building. Framing a roof may seem intimidating, but with proper planning and step-by-step execution, you can construct a sound, weather-resistant roof system. In this chapter, we'll cover the ins and outs of roof framing, from layout principles, and rafter calculations, to choosing materials and building complex roof shapes.

First things first – roof framing starts with thoughtful design. The roof pitch, or slope, dramatically impacts aesthetic style and functionality. We'll explore how to select the ideal pitch for snow load capacity, drainage, and architectural look. Get ready to rise to new heights! Pun intended. Once the pitch is decided, we'll choose between truss and rafter systems. Trusses enable wide-open cathedral ceilings, while rafters allow more customization. We'll calculate the needed lumber length and spacing, to carry loads properly.

Time to raise the roof! We'll hoist up the pre-built trusses with cranes, or lift stick-framed rafters into place, one by one. Seeing the roof structure take shape against the sky is a magical construction moment. We'll install collar ties and ridge boards to tie rafters together and give a surface for roof sheathing. With the skeleton up, we'll start layering on plywood or OSB sheathing. Proper water barriers, flashing, and ventilation baffles – it takes careful sequencing to weatherproof the roof.

Of course, we can't forget about building code compliance every step of the way, through permitting, engineered designs, and inspections. We'll ensure the roof framework meets wind, seismic, and snow load requirements so you can sleep soundly during storms! Beyond conventional gable roofs, we'll tackle more complex shapes like hips, valleys, dormers, and skylights. Vaults, turrets, mansards – don't be intimidated by fancy architectural vocabulary! With the right layout techniques, you can frame striking curvilinear roofs too. We'll strategize sturdy connections and structural supports so visually stunning roofs withstand nature's forces.

Calculating the rafter length and the roof's slope, or pitch, is pivotal to start planning. The pitch is measured as x inches of rise per 12 inches of horizontal run. A 4/12 slope means 4" of rise over a 12" run, while a steep 12/12 slope has 12" of rise per foot. Typically, pitches range between 3/12 and 12/12. What factors determine the ideal pitch? For snow country, steeper pitches in the 6/12 to 12/12 range, help snow slide off to prevent accumulation and roof collapse. In rainy climates, more slope aids drainage, to minimize leaks, mildew, and dripping eaves. Architectural style influences pitch, as well. Farmhouses should be around 6/12, bungalows 7/12 to 9/12, and sleek moderns sometimes as low as 3/12.

Let's calculate rafter the length based on the desired pitch. The roof slope triangle, helps determine the rafter's precise length. The horizontal run is half the width of your building, while the rise depends on the pitch. For example, a 24' wide house with a 6/12 pitch, has 12' run and 6' rise. Using the Pythagorean theorem, the hypotenuse rafter length is 13'. Always confirm length with plans and on-site measuring! For gable roofs, calculate the slope triangle, separately, for each side. Hip roofs involve more complex geometry. Beyond length, proper rafter angles are critical for an orderly roofline. That's where rafter squares and protractors are handy, to mark precise, angle cuts on rafter tails. A tight, neat roofline signals solid framing.

We'll walk you through rafter spacing next. Standard spacing is 16" on center, but wider at 24" can work for stretches without vertical load. Stagger joints between rafter layers for structural integrity. Don't forget to check code minimums too;many require doublers, under joints, to strengthen the framework. With correct length and spacing, our rafters will support the roof through all kinds of weather.

Now that pitch and slope are determined, let's choose our roof framing system. The two main options are trusses or rafters, stick-built on site. Trusses enable wide-open cathedral ceilings without interior load-bearing walls. The web of angled lumber creates strong triangular support. Attics are easier with rafters and ceiling joists, and allow customization like dormers.

Trusses must be engineered, to order, with exact lumber dimensions and metal gusset plates. Various designs suit different spans – talk through options with your truss manufacturer, early in planning. Once delivered, they can be quickly installed with cranes. Properly brace and reinforce all connections! Stick framing with regular rafters involves more work, but allows flexibility. We'll construct collar ties, ceiling joists, and ridge boards on-site. This also lets us integrate dormers, skylights, and custom elements. Stick framing requires skilled carpentry, with attentive cuts and connections. We'll go over timber joinery techniques, like fishplate reinforcements.

Material choices are key too. Dimensional lumber, up to 2x12s, can span shorter distances. Engineered lumber is stronger and resists warping. For long spans or special architecture, steel beams work with wood infill. We'll follow best practices for moisture control, so all materials perform optimally. Bonus tip: Consider supplementing standard framing with SIP panels! Structural insulated panels integrate insulation and sheathing with framing for strength. We can strategically use SIPs while stick-framing other areas. The combo yields high performance and flexibility.

Now, let's walk through the rafter framing process from start to finish. After laying the roof slope triangle, we'll establish an overhang distance. Standard is 12", but expand to 18-24" for more shade and weather protection. Mark rafter positions with chalk lines on the top wall plates. Cut pattern rafters with precisely angled, bird's mouth joints, ready for test fitting. Nail together a ridge board, straight and true, to align the roof peaks. Install rafters one by one, temporarily bracing the ends. The first few are the most challenging, so go slowly and check plumb angles.

We'll connect rafters with collar ties about halfway down for lateral stability. Use metal joist hangers for secure fastening. Measure equal lengths on each side to keep the roof symmetrical. Use increasingly longer rafters, moving out towards the eaves. The birds' mouth notch should rest flush on the top wall plate. At the peak, follow the ridge board angle for tight joinery. Use wood gussets, nailed in triangles, to reinforce the connections. We'll discuss various framing joints like fishplates and finger joints for extra strength. Once all common rafters are in place, it's time for the jack rafters. These shorter rafters fit on either side of the ridge to complete the roof. Cut jack lengths precisely, to sit flush with the ridge board angle. Glue for adhesion and nail off securely.

Let's check for a properly aligned roofline with equal overhangs before sheathing. Fix any high spots, now, to prevent future sagging. Install lookouts around the perimeter to strengthen overhanging rafter tails. We're almost ready to start weatherproofing this roof! When all structural framing components are securely in place, we can start layering on the protective roof sheathing. This decking goes beneath shingles or other roofing material. Two common options are plywood and oriented strand board (OSB). Let's compare the pros and cons.

Plywood has been around for decades with proven durability. It resists warping better than OSB. Costs are higher, but compensated by plywood's long lifespan. Go with 3/4" CDX pressure-treated boards for best weather protection. Watch for soft spots or delamination. OSB is engineered from wood chips and adhesive resins. It's more affordable but doesn't handle moisture as well. Still, modern manufacturing has improved water resistance. Stick with thicker 7/16" or 1/2" OSB for roofs. Avoid swollen or warped boards.

Next comes sheathing at the eaves, to provide an initial water barrier. Overlap seams and stagger joints between rows. This strengthens the sheet and minimizes leakage points. Use longer 8' x 4' sheets, to reduce seams. Nail 6" on center around the perimeter and 12" OC in the field. Pay special attention to weatherproofing valleys, ridges, and eaves. We'll install a peel-and-stick membrane, along with metal drip edge flashing, for the first line of defense against wind-driven rain. Proper shingle overhang into gutters also prevents water infiltration.

Ventilation is critical too! We need airflow from eave intakes, to ridge vents, to prevent condensation buildup. We'll look at how to install soffit vents, ventilation baffles, and louver vents, cleanly, into the framing plan. A well-vented roof stays drier longer. Inspect all flashing around roof protrusions, like chimneys and skylights, once sheathed. We'll seal any fishmouth gaps in the membrane, with high-quality caulk. Don't forget the weather barrier underlayer, too, before shingling. Building an airtight, watertight roof takes diligence – but the result is well worth it.

No roof is complete without character-giving accents. Dormers, turrets, cupolas, and other elevated features enhance architecture while letting in light. Let's go through best practices for framing attention-grabbing roof details. From concept to completion, we'll build eye-catching forms that function.

Dormers top the list for expanding living space and views. We can frame functional dormers in gable, hipped, or shed styles. Start by planning size, shape, and location – consider sight lines and snow load. Cut the roof opening carefully to the rafters and sheathing. Build dormer sidewalls, similar to regular walls, with double top plates and adequate headers. Install a sloped roof, mimicking the main roof pitch and overhang, for proportionality. Integrate siding, trim, and windows, attractively, with the rest of the house.

For round turrets, plan structural supports, like knee brackets, between floors. Cut rafter templates and a central turret cap frame. Lay out the turret roof slope, with overhangs barred for security. Maintain drainage gaps between the turret and the main roof, and in the end, you will see the charm is worth the careful framing.

Cupolas can evolve from simple decorative caps, to intricate miniature buildings. Frame multi-sided bases to match roof slopes, then install windows all around. Construct a miniature rafter roof, capped by a spire element. Adhere closely to code for railings and structural connections up high.

When it comes to towers, the sky's the limit – literally! Plan robust foundations and steel-reinforced framing to support multi-story heights. Consider open-air observation decks capped by a conical roof with 360° views. We'll angle stable, sweeping braces between the tower and the main building. These elevated elements require creative framing solutions. But, with some geometric ingenuity, we can build beautiful architecture that seems to defy gravity. Those soaring peaks will be functional and safe, thanks to the detail-oriented framework hidden underneath.

Roofs, especially on larger buildings, often involve intersecting shapes and directional changes. The transitions between roof sections require precise framing, especially vulnerable to leaks. Let's review how to frame graceful hips, valleys, and other joints smoothly and water-tight. Valleys are the inner corners where two roof sections meet in a "V" shape. Maintain a continuous valley rafter, along the junction, by angle-cutting the abutting rafters. Overlap shingles for water runoff . We'll reinforce the valley with flashing underneath. Hip ridges rise where roof planes join together in a shared outside corner, rather than intersecting. Calculate and cut hip rafters as longer diagonal members. Nail hip boards, over the joined hip rafter end, for a clean look. This helps divert water to perimeter eaves.

For more complex roofs, plan box valleys with cricket diverters and saddle flashings, to bridge multi-way intersections. Careful ductwork and vent placement, maintains airflow through hips and valleys. We want no rain or condensation pooling! If needed, build crickets behind chimneys and other roof protrusions, to divert water. Starting from the top down, frame a mini-roof to shield vulnerable spots. Include ample sloped sheathing, underlayment, and counterflashing. Don't forget detailing, like rake board fascia, along gable ends. We'll frame decorative shadow, barge, and crown molding for extra elegance. These special touches make the difference between a basic shed and an architectural showpiece! Let the unique angles and slopes of your roof guide framing creativity.

Beyond routine rectangles, a curved or vaulted roof makes a dramatic design statement. These aesthetically pleasing shapes require flexible framing techniques and lateral bracing. With smart layout and scrap lumber prototyping, you can frame sweeping, curved forms from scratch. Shallow vaults work with standard trusses, modified with angled top chords. Have steel splines custom-fabricated to achieve the desired curve profile. Anchor the splines securely to the top chords to tie the trusses together. Sheath the curves smoothly for graceful lines. For deeper curves, laminate flexible 1" thick boards to shape wooden ribs. Anchor ribs closely together along the vaulted ceiling line. Inflexible lumber can also be kerfed – sliced nearly through – to bend into shape. A strong connecting framework along the base and ridge ties it all together. Round structures need true arch framing with angled, wedge-shaped rafters. Lay out the curve perimeter with temporary center support. Test-fit-shaped rafter couples nailed together at the top. Once all pieces are cut and labeled, assemble the arch permanently.

Domes begin with a perimeter ring beam. Build curved ribs up to a round skylight cap. X-bracing and exterior sheathing will strengthen the spherical shape – laminated panels work great here. We'll waterproof it with a flexible membrane under shingles. There's something magical about raising curved frames against blue sky. That first arch taking shape will make all the careful cutoff and setup worthwhile. Don't be intimidated to try complex roof shapes with the right techniques. Let your imagination soar!

Once sheathing encloses the house, it's time to "dry in" and protect it from the weather. We'll bring in roofers to install waterproof underlayment, drip edge, and shingles, per code. Don't forget attic fireproofing before insulation! Coordinate scaffolding removal once shingles are down. Next we'll schedule window and exterior door installation, so openings are covered. Remember the sill pan flashing! The goal is to make the building envelope rain-tight, so interior work can proceed. Gutters and drainage should be functioning now too. Inspect waterproofing details, like chimney crickets, roof-to-wall intersections, and skylights for any weak spots. Touch up caulking and seals throughout. This is the best time for corrections, before walls and ceilings close up the evidence! Air sealing will improve efficiency and moisture resistance as well.

When water-tightness is satisfactory, we can move on to insulation, drywall, plumbing and electromechanically. But, make sure to photograph your pristine roof framing before it disappears from view! You'll look back proudly at the craftsmanship accomplished in these chapters. After these steps have been completed, you'll have a fully framed roof ready for the storm. With smart planning and a step-by-step process, you now have the skills to build roofs from simple to stunning. Just remember, every great building begins with a framework. When the foundation is solid, the structure can soar to new heights. Let's keep building!

Chapter 5

Building Stairs - Layout, Stringers, Treads, and Risers

You've framed up the floors and walls, put a roof overhead, and now it's time for the stairs - that gracefully sloped passageway that connects it all together. Get ready to ascend stair construction to new heights! Whether you're framing a basic straight staircase or an elaborate multi-level showpiece, the right techniques will help you rise to the challenge.

In this chapter we'll start from the bottom up, learning how to layout and build basic stair components, like stringers, treads and risers. We'll cover fundamental math, like calculating the ideal stair slope and dimensions. Proper layout is critical, so we'll demonstrate how to accurately mark and cut stringers, to avoid costly mistakes. Once you've mastered simple straight and L-shaped designs, we'll tackle more advanced staircase forms, like curving, flared, and split stairs. We'll build landings and integrate intricate details, like custom balustrades, handrails and trim work. You will learn professional secrets for framing sturdy, seamless stairs any decorator would envy. When you stand back and admire the finished staircase, you'll appreciate all the care and craftsmanship invested in its construction. Whether winding gracefully or striking a bold angular statement, these framed steps epitomize function and style. Get ready to gain serious stair wisdom!

Before we start cutting and assembling, it's important to understand the anatomy of a basic staircase and how the components fit together. The fundamental parts include the stringers, treads, risers, landings, handrails, and balusters. The stringers act as the structural "backbone" that provide underlying support for the stairs. Usually, 2–3 stringers are used in standard stair construction. Stringers have angled notches, cut into them, to hold each step. The treads are the horizontal boards you step on when climbing the stairs. The risers are the vertical boards in between each tread that connect them. Optional landings provide flat, rest areas between stair sections. These allow you to take a break mid-flight on long flights of stairs. Handrails are railings mounted on one or both sides of the stairs, for safety and support. Balusters are vertical members that fill in under the handrails.

Once you understand how the stringers, treads, risers, landings, handrails, and balusters all fit together, you can properly construct a staircase that is durable, safe, and aesthetically pleasing. It's important to build it right from the start, as minor defects in framing may go unnoticed, initially, but could compromise the stairs' safety and longevity down the road. Let's keep these key components in mind as we move forward.

The stringers bear the most weight and structural responsibility, transmitting loads safely down to the floor system. Though complex-looking, stringers simply comprise a series of angled cuts, corresponding to the tread and riser positions. We'll show you how to carefully lay out and cut sturdy stringers. For a straight-run staircase, you'll need a minimum of three stringers, though four is better. One stringer can be notched for installing treads and risers. The other two are left intact for strength. Hardwoods, like oak, are ideal, but pine works too if it's thick enough.

First, establish the total "rise" of the stairs, measuring from the floor of the upper level, down to the floor of the lower level. Next, following the code, determine an optimal "run" length based on the rise, adjusting the run to give a comfortable stair slope between 30–40 degrees. For example, say your total rise is 96". Dividing by a slope of 36 degrees gives a run of 144". That means each step should have a 12" tread depth and 7" riser height. Use these dimensions to mark the angles on the stringer.

Now comes the fun part - shaping the notches. I like to tackle the bottom cut, first, using a circular saw. Set the depth only 1/8" above the tread mark to leave a tiny notch lip. Work up the stringer, cutting each tread notch. Go slowly - one slip-up throws everything off! With notches complete, make identical cutouts on two more stringers. Place them 16" apart and interlock with floor joists. Install "L" brackets, glue, and screws for rock-solid connections. If desired, add blocking between stringers for extra strength. Once stringers are installed securely, you're ready to start installing treads and risers. Enjoy watching your staircase take shape stair by stair!

With stringers in place, it's time to infill with treads and risers. Getting these components square, plumb, and aligned makes the stairs safe and visually pleasing. Let's step through best practices for flawless fabrication and installation. Typical tread depths are 10-12," to easily accommodate most feet. Deeper treads can extend up to 24" for a luxurious feel underfoot. For risers, target 7-8" in height. Building codes limit the height to no more than 7 3/4" between floors. Studies show 7-inch risers create the most comfortable stride.

For sturdy treads on wood stairs, hardwoods like red oak and maple, are ideal, giving a handsome look that's easy to refinish. Standard 1" thick boards are suitable for straight runs. Curved or flared stairs demand thicker 1 1/4" treads for sufficient strength. Install treads, first, so their overhang creates a built-in platform for mounting risers. Carefully measure and mark each tread to fit stringer notches. Miter cutting tread ends at a 45-degree angle and ensures tight seams where treads meet. Cut notches to accommodate balusters if desired. Apply wood glue on stringers, then nail treads into place, through the top front edge only. For risers, measure between installed treads and cut boards, to create a snug fit. Nail upward, from underneath, where possible, or toenail into stringers. Careful workmanship ensures risers are perfectly plumb, with no gaps that could catch toes or shoes! Add wood filler, if needed, for seamless transitions between treads and risers.

The finishing touch is selecting attractive tread materials that complement your décor. For a contemporary look, choose exotic woods, stone, or metal materials. Play with color and grain patterns, or inset custom medallions, at each tread edge, for a personalized punch. Your stair treads make a design statement, so have fun playing designer!

On long or complex stairs, landings provide a welcome respite and safe transition point. After 12–16 stairs, building codes actually require a landing, to break up the run. Even when not mandated, strategic landings simplify framing and improve flow. Let's explore smart placement and construction tips. Landings can be designed, mid-staircase, between floors, or as starter platforms at the top or bottom. Size them at least as wide and deep as the stairs for maneuvering comfort and visual continuity. Large landings invite people to pause and converse, while narrow ones simply offer a quick breather space. For starters, frame the perimeter with doubled-up joists and headers, just like floor framing. Overlap joists with main floor systems, so loads transfer directly. Sheath the landing with sturdy 3/4-inch plywood underlayment, screwed into joists. Hardwood flooring or tile finishes are great for durability and aesthetics.

Check that landings are perfectly level to prevent trips and falls. Strive for less than 1/8-inch variation across the floor. Verify the landing sits square with stair runs using diagonal measurements. When framing walls around landings, plumb and straighten them meticulously. Landings open up creative possibilities too. Wrap open railings around landings to maintain light and airy spacing. Frame wide picture windows onto landings to usher in scenic views. Or, shape a cozy reading nook into the landing area. However you configure them, landings make stairs safer and give your legs a break!

What's a staircase without a beautifully crafted railing to guide the way? Don't neglect this essential safety feature and decorative accent. Study railing fundamentals, and you'll learn to frame custom railings even design aficionados admire. Railings serve the practical purpose of preventing falls and providing a sturdy handhold. Building codes dictate a minimum height of 36 inches for required railings. For added safety, frame 42-inch-high railings, if overlooking a room below. Graspable handrails should sit 34–38 inches above each tread nosing. While meeting code requirements, thoughtfully designed railings also enhance a staircase's style. Mix materials, like wrought iron balusters with oak handrails, for contrast. Frame custom molding profiles. Introduce creative flourishes like carved newel posts or ornamental baluster patterns. The design options are limitless!

Construct a sturdy base by mounting vertical baluster posts into the floor and ceiling. Space posts no more than 6 feet apart. Notch posts to accept crossbeams, called rails, then toenail everything together securely. Predrill holes for balusters to prevent splitting. For balusters themselves, choose strong, handsome wood species that take detail work well. Spacing between 4–6 inches prevents children from slipping through. Vary baluster styles - plain, twisted, or fluted - for textural intrigue. Don't overlook the handrail, which gets the most handling. Select durable, comfort-shaped wood. Think beyond basic wood railings, too. Mix in cable infill for lightness and transparency. Frame glass panel sections for protected viewing. The design is in your hands - have fun playing with shapes and details to make your staircase uniquely you. Those rails are more than just safety measures - they display your personal style!

If you're framing an open, expansive home, straight rectangular stairs would look rigid and out of place. Introduce flowing, curved designs to echo gentle contours and smooth traffic flow. Though curving stairs require more effort to frame, the eye-catching results are worth it! Before picking up any tools, sketch concepts to visualize the ideal curvature and placement. Calculate the arc radius by laying string tacked to the centers of the top and bottom treads. A 4-6 foot radius looks gracefully rounded without getting too tight. Larger radii, up to 12 feet, feel subtly curved. Now use the full-scale drawing to carefully cut a curved 2x12 to match the string's arc. Transfer the shape to your stringers one by one using a pattern bit on the router. For broad, gradual curves, kerf-cut the back of the stringer to help it bend smoothly into shape.

With stringers formed, mark and cut each tread to fit the curved notches. A tablesaw taper jig, makes quick work of this. Custom-cut every piece, as off-the-shelf treads won't match the arc. Risers can use stock boards cut shorter as needed. Tack components gradually, triple-checking alignment before nailing. For flared stairs, cut the stringers so they widen gracefully on one end. This opens up a staircase visually, directing the eye where you desire. Sweeten the flare with shapely rounded nosings, ornamental newel posts, and a robust landing frame. Floating treads on minimalist steel rods create a light, suspended effect. Dream big with those curving creations!

Once you've mastered straight and curved stairs, it's time for advanced geometries, like winders, spirals, and split designs. These unique stairs make navigating multi-story spaces a design adventure! Though complicated to build, innovative framing know-how, turns the complexity into carpentry bragging rights.

Winders are great when you need to make tight 180-degree turns within a compact footprint. Essentially, winders wedge triangular "pie slices" between tapered stringers that radiate from a center post. It takes math finesse to calculate exact angles and cut stringers. Precisely aligned, winders result in a smooth, continuous passage without any uneven risers or treads. Spiral stairs are the ultimate space-saver, winding elliptically in a tight circle surrounding a column. They can be elaborately decorative too with custom metalwork and railings. But the reason most people save this for advanced framers is the tricky process of bending and joining stringers into a continuous coil. Each tread and riser must align precisely with the next for safety. A miscalculation means re-cutting the entire spiral - so double check measurements! Split stairs change direction mid-run, often with a half landing built-in. Picture two opposing L-shaped flights connected by a platform. This lets stairs turn back on themselves within a compact area. The tricky part is framing split stringers with intricately angled cuts, at the splitting mid-section. But, the beauty, when complete, is striking. Give your guests a mental and visual delight!

However you choose to show off your framing skills through unconventional stairs, the awe factor makes the extra effort worthwhile. Just take the geometry step-by-step and remember - measure twice, cut once! Patience and precision combines artsy form with sound function. Integrating Creative Touches & Safety Details beyond fundamental framing, the lumber options are wide open for infusing decorative accents and safety features into your staircase design. Take inspiration from these creative integrations to make stairs uniquely your own:

Underlighting - Set off each tread with radiant downlighting or mini LED strips for a dramatic glowing effect.
Contrasting Inlays - Frame a contrasting wood accent strip into tread edges for definition.
Hidden Storage - Outfit risers or open side areas with discreet storage compartments.
Tactile Handrails - Shape ergonomic, tactile handrail profiles for comfort and character.
Retractable Gates - At the top and bottom, install swing-away gates to prevent falls.
Antislip Treads - Adhere grip tape strips to tread edges or use textured tread materials.

Motion Sensors - For convenience and safety, install tread lights that react to movement.

Reading Nooks - Carve out small, recessed spaces along the sides.

Themed Treads - Have fun with colorful carpet runners or decorate treads with mosaic themes.

Let your inner designer run wild! When it comes to staircases, anything goes. Integrate safety and function, then dress it up with aesthetic details that delight. Think outside the box and discover inspiring new ways to personalize this pivotal passageway.

Before attempting that first climb, it's crucial to thoroughly inspect your framing work and confirm everything is structurally sound. Safety issues, like loose connections, uneven surfaces, and omitted handrails could cause serious accidents. So, let's equip ourselves with inspection checklists to catch any defects before opening the staircase for use. Start by verifying that your calculated dimensions adhere to applicable building codes for tread depth, riser height, railing height, and more. Confirm the angles don't exceed 30-40 degrees. Inspect spacing between balusters, spindles, and railing infill - no more than 6 inches is allowed. Next, carefully check every framing connection, juncture, and fastener. Are stringers securely attached to the floor systems above and below? Do balusters connect snugly with proper nails and screws? Are handrails tightly grasped by baluster posts and newel posts? Even minor looseness compromises integrity. Scan for any splits, cracks, knots, or defects in the wood framing. Look for uneven treads, corner gaps between risers, and other spots where someone could potentially catch a shoe and trip. Sand any rough spots, listen for creaks, and add blocking, if needed, to stiffen treads.

Finally, thoroughly clean the stairs before use. Vacuum up stray sawdust and wipe down woodwork. Once everything looks pristine, invite family members to test out the stairs and give feedback. Ask them to lean and push on the railings to check for any looseness. Only when everyone agrees the stairs are solidly constructed and safe should you officially open the passage! Your stairway framing skills have officially reached new heights! Whether a simple straight shot or an elaborate spiral structure, you now have the knowledge to take those stairs to the next level. Let your imagination soar, then make it a reality, one meticulously cut stringer at a time. Just take it step-by-step. Before you know it, you'll be at the top, admiring the view!

Now that you're a stair-framing master, it's time to move on and learn about installing windows and doors. Proper framing allows you to hang doors perfectly plumb and craft custom window sills and headers with ease. Moving on from stairs to windows is a logical progression as we shift focus to the home's exterior shell. So, grab your T-square and let's frame some windows! The dazzling views are just around the corner in Chapter 6.

Chapter 6

Installing Windows and Exterior Doors

Selecting the right windows and doors is critical for both the aesthetics and performance of your home. Beautiful bay windows usher in sunlight to brighten up a room, while a charming Dutch door adds old-world character to a kitchen. Energy-efficient models keep heating and cooling costs down, while sturdy designs withstand weather and improve security. With so many options to pick from, it can get overwhelming to find the perfect windows and doors for your new build. But have no fear, we'll break it all down step-by-step in this handy chapter! We'll cover how to choose styles and materials that suit your home's design and climate. This guide will explain the difference between various glazing, operable types, hardware, and other key features. We'll dive into structural considerations, for properly framing openings to bear weight and shed water.

Once decisions are made, we'll focus on proper installation techniques. I'll demonstrate how to flash, seal, shim, and anchor windows for optimal performance and longevity. You'll gain confidence cutting precision openings, integrating weather barriers, and trimming out a professional-looking finish. We'll also review best practices for hanging exterior doors, aligning hinges, and troubleshooting any sticking or sealing issues. Follow along as we assess your existing windows and doors to determine whether refurbishing or replacing makes more sense. Learn how to remove old units safely and prep the rough opening for fresh installs. Whether your project is a simple powder room door swap, or a whole house window overhaul, this chapter will equip you with expert skills. Let's begin exploring the wide, wonderful world of windows and doors!

The first big consideration is what styles and types of windows to use in each part of your home. Picture those dreamy corner windows overflowing with potted plants in the breakfast nook, or a stately French door welcoming guests by the front entry. Placement and design play a starring role in your home's personality. Let's discuss how to select windows to "fit the face" of your facade and interior spaces.

Double-hung windows are a classic choice, with two sashes that slide up and down for ventilation. They're easy to open and clean and have a traditional divided-lite look. For modern simplicity, opt for fixed picture windows arranged in clean lines. Add awning or hopper windows, to catch breezes above and below. Sliding windows save space with horizontally gliding sashes, and for unique architectural flair, choose rounded, arched, or angled windows.

If your style leans contemporary, sleek, floor-to-ceiling windows make a dramatic statement. These maximize views and add daylight, while emphasizing clean lines. For a more welcoming cottage or craftsman feel, go for smaller, divided lite windows with trim. Play with mixing and matching shapes and styles between rooms. A bold geometric window, punctuating a minimalist living space, can be striking.

Beyond aesthetics, carefully consider functionality for each window location. Bathrooms, for instance, need ventilation and privacy. Skylights shower interiors with natural light, and picture windows take center stage in living rooms. Bedrooms, situated above ground level, often benefit from egress windows for emergency exit or rescue access. Also, it's good to remember, warm southern exposures, call for shading devices like overhangs or screened porches.

Now let's explore common window operation types, so you can decide which suits each application. Double or single hung windows are most popular for their easy up-down sliding, sash operation. Awning style windows hinge at the top and tip outward, controlling air flow, even during storms or rain. Hopper windows are the reverse, hinged at the bottom to push inward. Sliding windows glide horizontally on tracks, saving space with no swinging sash. Casement windows crank open to the side, funneling in air. Fixed picture windows offer no ventilation but provide the greatest unobstructed views. Specialty types like bay, garden, and tilt-turn windows enhance function in unique spaces. Within these operation styles, you'll also choose between various energy-efficient glazing options. Double-pane insulated glass minimizes heat transfer for superior insulation. Low-emissivity coatings on glass, reflect radiant heat to keep interiors cozy. Triple pane windows take it a step further for R-value up to R-10,and for balmy climates, impact-resistant, laminated glass protects against storms and security breaches.

As for doors, there are many options for blessing your home with beauty, security, and charm. We'll start with the grand entrance, making first impressions. Classical wood doors with decorative glass shout welcome, while sleek steel designs telegraph modern elegance. Glass inserts not only bathe foyers with light, but also reveal your front yard haven to approaching guests. For durability and weather resistance, fiberglass and steel doors are top performers. Look for solid wood edges with composite or foam core construction that resists rotting and warping. Thermal breaks also improve efficiency by stopping conductive heat flow. Adjustable sill systems make aligning and sealing doors a breeze during installation.

Beyond the entry, doors must suit function and access in each space. For wide-open concept plans, pocket doors slide discreetly into walls to conserve square footage. They're ideal for master suites and powder rooms, too. French doors lend old-world sophistication to patios, libraries, and bedrooms. Roll-up garage doors provide everyday access plus ventilation. Barn-style sliding doors are trendy space savers that glide smoothly on ceiling-mounted tracks. Their clean lined industrial vibe works in farmhouses, loft, and modern settings. Dutch doors split in half to welcome breezes while keeping pets in and children out, and high impact hurricane doors stand guard in coastal climates when storms come calling.

Clearly, those gorgeous glossy ads capture just a fraction of the possibilities! Before finalizing any decisions, be sure to evaluate the structural requirements for the windows and doors you're considering. Let's go over some key framing factors that impact size, weight, load path, and integrations, with other building systems.

First, take a look at your floor plan blueprint, sections, and elevations. Where are large openings, like sliding glass walls or multi-panel patio doors, shown? How about big bay windows - are they bumped out or inset? This will determine how much load the surrounding framing can handle. If windows and doors are placed above one another vertically, loads stack up and increase. Factor in wall type, too. Load bearing walls need appropriately sized headers to transfer weight from above to studs below. Headers may span openings directly or support intermediate posts or beams. Non-load bearing walls have more framing flexibility. Also, examine any intersecting wall joints, keeping the double top plate or overlapping studs intact for continuity.

Now let's talk about shear walls, a critical element of the seismic force resisting system. Shear walls resist lateral earthquake and wind forces, using stiff structural panels. Limit window and door penetration of designated shear walls to 25% of the wall length minimum, and install hold down anchors tying shear walls securely to foundation and framing. While we're looking at shear wall locations, also check for any long expanses of windows on the plans. These should have shear transfer connections to strengthen the perimeter framing against racking from wind pressure. Use tie-downs, clips, and blocking to integrate segments, so the wall performs as one unit. At sloped ceilings, roof to wall step-downs, or advanced framing corners, ensure proper load transfer between intersecting members. Corners and openings are common failure points, so inspect structural plans for the architect's intended load path. Don't just lop off a stud without support - replace it with jack studs and headers sized for the roof above.

Are there bay windows or bonus rooms over garages in your floor plan? The framing details become more intricate, as loads get heavier. Foundation stem walls must extend, with piers potentially added beneath. The ceiling below, needs beams thick enough for the cantilevered weight, and roof rafters or trusses anchor tightly, into a reinforced band or rim joist. While surveying the plans, also check for any skylights or roof windows specified. These nifty devices funnel sunbeams into interior zones, but require careful waterproofing details, which we'll cover shortly. Roof structure needs reinforcing to span the opening, and ceiling joists must link rigidly to valley or hip ridge beams.

Across the facade, scan for any continuous band or ribbon windows planned. These look sleek but interrupt wall framing, so strong headers and sill plates tie it together. Weep holes for drainage, proper flashing, and thick exterior wall insulation, also prevent moisture issues. This keeps your ultra-modern exterior inviting, not leaking!

For doors, analyze your layout to position them in places that make sense spatially, without compromising wall structure. They require doubled up studs for jamb backing, supporting the frame header, and bolt-through hardware hinges. Coordinate door placement with mechanical systems, too, keeping ducts and vents away from potential conflicts.

That covers the structural considerations - great job! Thoughtful planning now, will ensure your windows and doors integrate seamlessly into well articulated framing. Next, let's get down to the nitty-gritty installation steps for creating perfect wall openings onsite. We'll go over everything from safe demo and prep to integrating flashings and weather barriers, for airtight, durable results.

If your project involves replacing existing windows or doors, we'll first need to carefully remove the old units. Start by prepping the interior space, laying protective drop cloths, and clearing any furnishings or curtains out of work range. For replacement while homeowners are still living there, install temporary particle board panels to cover openings at night. When you're ready to begin removal, use a utility knife to score caulking joints around the interior trim. Remove any jamb or stop molding first, taking care not to gouge the surrounding walls. Use a pry bar and hammer to pull nails from the exterior casing gradually. Removing elements in this order prevents damage. Wedge shims around the perimeter to relieve pressure as you work.

With all trim work detached, examine how the unit is affixed in the opening. Older windows may be nailed directly, but newer installs use screws into surrounding shims and blocking. Locate all fasteners and remove them systematically while supporting the weight. On the exterior, cut any sealants with an oscillating saw before prying the framework loose. Have an assistant support the window from the inside as you work. Once completely loosened, carry the intact window outside for disposal, being extremely careful not to drop broken glass. Take care to keep the existing flashing, waterproof membrane and sheathing undamaged if possible. Back inside, assess the rough opening condition. Are the studs rotted or damaged? Any gaps, cracks or rodents to contend with? Address issues, now, before installation. Check for level and plumb, and make any adjustments needed to square the frame. Cut back protruding stud fingers and vacuum debris before covering with protective sheathing temporarily.

For new construction installs, ensure openings are precisely positioned on prints and correctly oriented, then framed to exact measurements. King and jack studs should be straight, and double up jamb studs where hinges will mount. Remember to accommodate shim space and flashing when sizing rough openings. This helps avoid problems down the road.

Before setting the new unit, do a trial fit by setting it into place and examining the gap perimeter for consistency. Make any final adjustments to shim spacing needed for a smooth fit. Also, confirm the window remains square without racking when partially fastened. If any issue, reposition jack studs and re-check until satisfied. Proper, rough opening setup prevents leaks and headaches down the road. Now, prep for airtight, watertight installation using flashing and barrier membranes. For windows, flexible self-adhered flashing strips go down first. Apply at sill, then jambs, installing behind the nailing flange, to divert water out. Make diagonal relief cuts, at corners, to fold together snugly. On top of this, the weather resistive barrier, or building wrap, seals against air infiltration. Paper-faced wraps need sealing tape, while some self-adhere. Prime surfaces, first, for max bond. Overlap at least 6 inches onto the window perimeter. Fully covered openings prevent drafts and moisture entry.

For doors, the technique is similar but modified. The sill area takes an L-shaped pan flashing underneath, with membrane covering it. Jamb flashings have flanges that slip behind the weather barrier. Use spray foam or mastic, at flashing seams, for full seal. Proper flashing integration makes a lasting difference.

Now set the unit plumb, level, and square in the prepared opening. We'll use shims spaced every 6 to 8 inches around the sides to stabilize and fill voids. Don't distort the frame or force it out of position. Adjust shims gradually until satisfied with alignment. Then screw through jambs, into shims or studs, to secure in place. Depending on window type, full perimeter nailing flanges may be available . If so, attach through the flange, into sheathing and framing, using the manufacturer's specified fastener pattern. Where no flange exists, we'll anchor into the jamb backing instead. This provides structural stability in high wind zones.

Next comes waterproof, flexible exterior sealant application around the full unit perimeter. Tool the sealant with a round shape, 90-degree angle for cleanest finish. Sealants stick to the flashing, sheathing, and unit frame to create a gasket that directs water downward. Caulk offers the first line of defense against moisture. The interior side gets a bead of acrylic latex caulk at the gap between unit frame and drywall. This neatly covers any minor gaps from shims, providing aesthetic finish. Don't seal windows shut by accident, though! We need operable access for construction and air exchange to dry materials. It also facilitates inspection as we go. Double check function of the installed unit now. Window sashes and locking mechanisms should function smoothly. No blade binding or catch points should be an issue. Ensure clips, drives, and hardware connect properly. Door knobs, deadbolts, and strikes align precisely when closed. Issues are much simpler to address, before, interior trim finishes.

Let's turn to trimming out openings to finalize the polished interior look. Use a laser level to trace cutting lines for straight, clean results. Miter corners to precise angles - Edges meet flush with no gaps. On windows, install interior stops or Liner panels, to cover shims and finishing gaps. This creates a neat, integrated appearance. Carefully measure and cut exterior casing or brick molding to overlap siding at the correct width. Maintain alignment of corners. Adhere with nails and sealant to protect from moisture entry. Slope the sill piece slightly outward to direct runoff away from the unit, and add architectural embellishments, like crown molding, for custom drama. Pre-drill and hand nail all trim to prevent splits, using galvanized or stainless steel finish nails. Countersink slightly and fill over holes for seamless results. Take care screwing into window frames - pre-drill and don't over tighten! Apply wood filler over nails and caulk at miters for professional finish. Add back interior stops or sills removed earlier.

Examine the trimmed opening from every angle, inside and out. All trim should lie flat and corners align evenly. Joints between components are sealed effectively against air and moisture penetration. Operable windows glide smoothly, and doors swing freely without rubbing. Your sleek finish will stand the test of time and weather! Resist the urge to seal windows completely closed just yet. During construction, air circulation helps dry out materials and mitigate moisture issues. Leave windows operable, except during storms, until interior paint and finishes cure. Then go ahead and seal the gap between the frame and rough opening, on both sides, for final insulated, airtight installation.

There you have it - well installed windows and doors breathe life into your home visually and functionally. They withstand weather securely to shelter your family for generations. Next, we'll move on to insulating this sturdy framing to keep interiors comfortably temperate. Proper insulation works hand in hand with high performance windows and doors

Chapter 7

Adding Interior Walls and Partitions

Interior walls and partitions are essential framing elements that transform an empty shell into a functional home, divided into livable spaces. While exterior walls withstand weather and support structural loads, interior framing creates versatility in layout. Walls define distinct rooms, like bedrooms, baths, and closets, while maintaining open flow in kitchens and living areas. Strategic placement turns lumber and drywall into the backdrop for your unique lifestyle.

Before grabbing a hammer, thoughtful planning ensures interior walls optimize both aesthetics and practicality. Consider traffic flow between spaces and how rooms will be furnished. Picture daily routines like cooking, reading, and lounging to dictate ideal room size and configuration. Lighting is key too - we'll place windows to brighten dark corners while allowing privacy as desired. Don't forget to account for plumbing and electrical; framing around these systems now prevents problems and headaches later. While dimensions and layout vary by design, the framing process remains the same. We'll follow a logical sequence starting with the fixed elements, like plumbing walls, then framing flexible dividing walls. We'll walk you through choosing lumber sizes, laying out studs, and constructing specialized framing, like arches and corners. With accurate cuts and secure connections, the bones of your new interior take shape. Soon these fundamental framing skills will feel like second nature!

Before the hammer hits the nail, safety comes first. Ensure adequate ventilation when cutting wood, wear eye and ear protection, and keep the site organized to prevent slips and falls. Proper lifting technique protects your back - recruit a buddy for heavy boards, and protect existing, finished areas from dust and damage as we frame up the new additions. Investing a little time to safeguard yourself and your home now, yields big dividends through years of enjoyment. Okay, tool belts buckled and blueprints in hand? Let's get framing! I suggest we start by outlining permanent interior walls like bathrooms. Precise plumbing layouts mean more measuring and cutting, but it's easiest to frame fixed components before erecting flexible room dividers. We'll construct any load-bearing walls, next, to transfer weight from the roof to the foundation. Only then will we frame partitions defining living spaces, like bedrooms and dens.

Time to pull out the ladder and tape measure! Marking stud layout requires accuracy down to a 1/16th inch. On load bearing walls, we'll use substantial 2x6 or 2x8 studs on 16" center spacings. Non-load bearing partitions only need 2x4s spaced 24" apart. Corners employ special framing to tie walls together sturdily. Where walls intersect, plan for additional jack and cripple studs, to maintain integrity and insulation. Wow, with studs marked, the framing bays look like dot-to-dot drawings! Now we're ready to align bottom plates and stand up the walls. I'll demonstrate proper lifting technique, so you don't hurt your back. With walls temporarily braced plumb, we can attach headers and sills to tie them together. Throw in some shear panels diagonally, and we've got a rigid, square framework.

Framing interior openings for doors and windows takes precise measuring, too. We need appropriately sized headers to transfer weight above openings. Arched tops require special curved framing - you'll learn a trick to trace these graceful curves. Jamb studs plumb the sides of openings, so doors and windows operate smoothly for decades. A solid sill below finishes the job.

Great work! Load-bearing and dividing walls are framed floor to ceiling, but now let's try some partial height partitions. These flexible barriers separate spaces, while allowing light and views between rooms. A pony wall divides zones subtly, while a half-wall makes a decorative railing anchor. We can frame custom counter height for bar areas as well. Now we're ready to integrate electrical and insulation before sheathing the walls. Careful wiring placement ensures every room has power and lighting, exactly where needed. Insulation deadens sound and sustains comfortable temperatures indoors.

Come along as I demonstrate strategies for air sealing gaps and installing insulation to specification. We want snug, draft-free rooms that hold heat in winter and stay cooler in summer. Saving energy keeps money in your pocket and reduces environmental impact too - it's a win-win. With framing complete up to the roofline, our interior shell is shaped and insulated. Next we'll apply exterior sheathing before roofing, then hang drywall throughout the interior. No more exposed skeleton! Installing drywall is satisfying after focusing on structural framing, and with some simple finishing techniques, drywall transforms into gorgeous, flat surfaces, ready for priming and painting. Nothing dresses up new construction like a fresh coat of color.

Drywall work stirs up fine particles, so keep that ventilator on. Stay hydrated too. Grab a straightedge to ensure seams land on studs, then we'll nail sheets in place with a specialized gun. I'll demonstrate how to properly tape joints for invisible, durable finishes. Don't rush the delicate sanding either - imperfections would haunt you forever under critical lighting. But with attention to detail, flawless drywall sets the stage for stunning interiors.

Paint may finish the walls, but doors and trim add functionality and style. Installing interior doors opens up new possibilities for privacy, noise control and architectural detail. We'll frame openings to exact dimensions, so doors operate smoothly. Jambs, stops, casings and sills all contribute to handsome finished openings. Beyond sheer utility, the right doors lend elegance and complement your home's character.While on the topic of trim, let's carve out time to craft those finishing touches that pull rooms together: cove molding, chair rail, wainscoting, baseboard and crown. Simple trim transforms boxy rooms into gracious, inviting spaces rich with detail. We'll construct built-in shelving and cabinets too for custom storage solutions. Your hands will gain precision cutting trim, and take pride seeing elegant details come to life room by room.

This framing knowledge empowers you to divide interior space however you see fit. With flexible wall placement options, the possibilities are endless! Maybe you'll frame signature arched doorways, an artistic window niche, or cozy reading alcoves. We've built the framing fundamentals, now get creative with layouts. Make bold choices - it's only wood and drywall, after all. Next, we'll work on constructing graceful stairs to make circulation through multi-level homes a breeze. Floating stringers and artful railings transform staircases from purely functional to breathtaking focal points. Measure twice, cut once is the rule though - missteps compound quickly! But, with care and patience, we'll construct stairs worthy of decades of foot traffic.

From mere lumber and nails, we've framed up walls to meet your exact living needs. With insulation, wiring and drywall, this shell becomes a comfortable sanctuary against the elements. When you look back on our work someday, remember the vision and labor that shaped your home at its core. May the memories made within these walls be as rock-solid as the framing that gives them form. Now those snug, smartly framed rooms need finishing touches to make them home. Next, we'll hang doors, install cabinets, and build out inspiring living spaces.

Doors and cabinets get all the glory, but humble trim is the unsung hero that truly perfects interior spaces. The baseboard, crown molding, chair rail, and wainscoting blend aesthetics and function brilliantly. Trim conceals messy edges, protects walls from scuffs, and accentuates architectural details. With plentiful styles to choose from, let's explore your options for elegantly trimming out the interior.

Baseboard is the fundamental trim encircling every room along the floor. It bridges gaps between floors and walls with a tidy finished edge. Simple, versatile baseboard suits traditional or modern spaces. Or, make a statement with a substantial, built-up baseboard carrying visual weight. Increase durability in high-traffic areas with extra beefy baseboard, built to handle bumps and scuffs. If the baseboard is the foundation, crown molding is the crowning glory, accentuating ceilings. Even a modest cove or stepped crown, lends rooms a polished, upscale look. Or, go bold with a substantial ornamental crown, mimicking opulent classical architecture. Miters seamlessly transition corners for museum-quality craftsmanship. Whatever profile fits your style, crown molding subtly catches the eye. For another graceful, horizontal accent, the chair rail sits just below shoulder height. Traditionally, it protected walls from chair backs while allowing contrasting colors above and below. Chair rails neatly divide walls visually, too. Use it to make a small room feel larger, or define dining and seating zones in open concept layouts. Perfectly horizontal and level chair rail screams sophistication.

Let's not overlook the vertical dimension, either. Wainscoting panels, framed with trim, add texture and depth to lower walls. Beadboard wainscoting lends vintage farmhouse charm in a breezy hallway. Formal, raised panel wainscoting contrasts elegantly with smooth upper walls in a dignified dining room. Arrange board and batten vertically for an outdoorsy, rustic aesthetic. Design options abound! Windows and doors demand intricate surrounding trim, as well. A basic window needs a well-fitted sill, apron, side casings, and header to look intentional. Boost the ambiance with thicker casings, sill nosing, under sill trim, or ornamental crowns. Doors gain character with nice casings, backbands, plinth blocks, or pediments topping the header. Careful mitering and precise coping make trim flow seamlessly, across angled transitions.

Beyond these essentials, don't limit your trim ambitions! Frame recessed niches for displaying art or relics. Build window seats and bookcases complete with shelving and cabinetry. Cozy window benches, flanking a bay window, make a peaceful reading nook. Construct a custom media center combining cabinets, niches, and shelving tailored to your components. With creative carpentry, the possibilities are truly endless.

Installing all this specialty trim is satisfying finish work after structural framing. But don't downplay the skills required. Trim carpentry demands patience, precision, and a keen spatial eye. Creating flawless lines and tight seams, challenges even seasoned carpenters. Measure carefully, never forcing pieces that don't fit. With practice, you'll become comfortable translating dimensions to neatly mitered trim.

Let's start our trim training with some simple baseboard installation. We'll use finish nails, driven through the tongue at an angle, into the studs. Where walls meet, precise coped joints beat basic butt joints. They conceal any gaps while showing off smooth, unbroken contours. Coping takes light hands and a sharp coping saw. It's time for inside corners, outside corners, and transitions. Pre-mitered corners make this quicker, or we can cut precision angles on-site. Where baseboard meets casings, blocks, or other trim, take time to notch and scribe for a custom fit. It only takes one jagged transition to detract from all our careful efforts. But, with practice, mitering and scribing become second nature.

.

Let's move on to crowning the room with distinguished molding, accentuating the ceiling. For a foolproof installation, hold planks against the ceiling and mark angle cuts. Nails driven upwards through the top edge attach it securely. Where outside corners meet, a neatly mitered seam upholds the illusion of continuity. Inside corners get a bit trickier. We'll cut wide bevels and ease the joint together, so the ceilings feel expansive.
To achieve reveals that match the room, rip strips of wood to consistent widths and tack them temporarily, as spacers. This allows us to position trim precisely before nailing. Custom radius profiles open up curvaceous options beyond basic straight cuts, and for long flawless runs, instead of nailing, adhesive offers an invisible attachment. Little details make all the difference!

Your newly gained skills unlock vast potential for customization. Any niche, shelf, cubby, or cranny you imagine, can now come to life! Building up a room's trim brings immense satisfaction. When installed properly, trim appears effortless and inevitable, as if walls were meant to be adorned this way. Trimis the jewelry that brings out the inner beauty and completes each space.

Now, let's discover the transformative power of cabinets. Beyond expanding storage, cabinetry introduces limitless design potential. Cabinets establish zones, like kitchens and pantries, while hiding necessities behind elegant facades. Freestanding cabinets make versatile room dividers too. With carefully planned built-ins, we can exploit every last bit of space efficiency. The frame-and-panel construction we've mastered transfers easily to cabinetry. We'll construct boxes from plywood and solid wood, making them as sturdy as our walls. Drawers, roll-outs, and adjustable shelving equip the interiors for your unique storage needs. Then, style the cabinet faces with complementary door styles and hardware that express your tastes. With vast design options, cabinets accommodate any aesthetic you desire. For a homey cottage kitchen, painted Shaker-style doors, add humble charm. Or, emulate old-world tradition with intricate raised panel doors and crown molding. Contemporary cabinets go slick with solid colors and integrated handles. Mix and match to strike the ideal balance for your home.

Beyond style, careful installation makes cabinets look and function like a dream. We'll shim boxes perfectly plumb and anchor them securely into studs. Drawers slide smoothly on hidden tracks, softly catching with self-closing mechanisms. Adjust shelves effortlessly along discrete metal channels. Thoughtful touches, like rollout trays and garbage cans, improve the everyday experience. Little motions become fluid rituals.

Transitioning from rough construction to fine finish work takes adjusting your methods. Quick cuts and hammer swings turn into slow, precise motions. Set aside impatience and let details unfold at their own pace. Stillness and focus replace hustle and force. Each joint, reveal, and adjustment inch the project toward perfection. Months of labor culminate in these finishing touches that fulfill your home's potential.

With trim fully installed and cabinets thoughtfully incorporated, we breathe life into once-empty rooms. Your choices direct form and function to suit how you want to live. Our hands manifest that vision through framing and finishing. Now these refined spaces invite your activities and routines day after day. May the walls hold your experiences close, keeping cherished memories safe from time's steady march. Bask in this milestone, and know that with each completed room, you're one step closer to enjoying your dream home.

Only one task remains to complete this chapter... installing doors! But that's a big job deserving fresh energy. Mark this major interior milestone in your mind. Then rest your body and let the anticipation build for the day we hang those doors and declare the interior finished. You're almost there! For now, admire your trimmed out rooms and know that with each accomplished project, you gain skills and confidence for the next. See you soon to hang those doors and transform this shell into a welcoming place you're proud to call home.

Chapter 8

Insulating the Frame - Staying Warm and Saving Energy

Insulating a home's framework is a critical step that too often gets overlooked by amateur builders. But, proper insulation is essential for energy efficiency, cost savings, comfort, and condensation control. As we insulate our framed walls, ceilings and floors, we'll delve into the science behind selecting the right materials and installing them correctly. Get ready to cozy up your construct with top-notch insulation techniques.

When designing a home, we must consider the entire thermal envelope and minimize any gaps in insulation coverage. Heat naturally wants to transfer from warmer areas to cooler ones until an equilibrium is reached. In winter, our heated indoor air tries to escape outwards, resulting in chilly rooms and high energy bills. Insulation creates resistance to heat flow, trapping warmth inside. Similarly, in summer, insulation blocks external heat from warming up our air-conditioned refuge. For comfortable living year-round, we need insulation sufficient to moderate heat transfer in both directions.

How does insulation actually slow heat transfer? There are three types of heat transfer in play: conduction, convection, and radiation. Conduction is direct heat flow through a solid material, like heat traveling through a frying pan handle. Insulation works by trapping tiny air pockets, limiting conductive heat flow. These trapped air pockets can't easily move, which also minimizes convection currents that carry heat. Finally, insulation's reflective properties provide radiant barriers that block infrared radiation. With all three forms of heat transfer obstructed, insulation keeps interior temperatures stable and comfortable.

Now that we understand the science of insulation, let's explore the different materials available. The optimal insulation type depends on factors like climate, budget, and construction style. We'll delve into the pros and cons of today's most common insulation materials so you can select the perfect fit.

Fiberglass insulation has been the status quo for decades thanks to its affordability and ease of installation. Made from melted sand and recycled glass, fiberglass forms fluffy batts, or loosefill that easily conform to framing cavities. It gets crammed between studs, joists, and rafters to limit air movement. Fiberglass does a decent job restricting heat conduction, and provides an R-value around R-3 per inch. The downsides are potential skin irritation during handling and sagging over time.

In recent years, mineral wool like Roxul has surged in popularity as a fiberglass alternative. Made from molten rock or slag, mineral wool batts, boast an R-value up to R-3.5 per inch. The rigid structure holds its shape in walls and ceilings with minimal sagging. Though mineral wool costs a bit more than fiberglass, it wins points for fire resistance and sound dampening. The high density deters settlement while damping noise between rooms. For green builders, mineral wool's natural material composition is a bonus too.

Next up, is rigid foam insulation, available in sheets of polystyrene or polyisocyanurate foam. Foam boards deliver an exceptional R-value of R-5 or more per inch, providing ample insulation in thinner applications. Use rigid foam to beef up R-values in exterior walls, unvented roofs, concrete slabs, and other unique construction assemblies. Foam's air-tight structure also seals thermal leaks for added efficiency. Drawbacks include cost and flammability concerns. Special fire-resistant variants, like ThermoPly, address these issues.

Want even higher performance from thinner insulation? Aerogel blankets and other vacuum insulated panels (VIPs) nearly eliminate convective and conductive heat transfer, thanks to their nanoporous structure. With up to R-30 insulation value per inch, VIPs enable compact, energy efficient constructions. However, the manufacturing process makes VIPs cost prohibitive for most builders. As production expands, keep an eye on this space-age, superinsulation option.

The next question - how much insulation is enough? Building codes set minimum R-values for insulation, based on climate, but we can exceed the code for maximum efficiency. Shoot for R-13 batts in exterior walls, R-30 in ceilings, and R-19 under floors. Up those values to R-15, R-38, and R-25 in colder northern regions for toasty warm homes. Here in the South, we often overlook floor insulation, since frost heave isn't a concern. But, even here in Georgia, insulating basement and crawlspace floors keep floors comfortably warm. I'll never forget working on a friend's lake house, built atop a vented crawl space. The floor was always chilly, even with the furnace blasting! After retrofitting with R-19 batts between the floor joists, he said it finally felt warm and homey, even on cold winter mornings. What a difference insulation makes!

Now that we've mapped our insulation plan for framed walls, ceilings, floors, and any tricky architectural details, it's time to move on to the next step. Let's fluff those batts and start packing insulation into each cavity! I like to use the bulkiest insulation that will fit, squeezing in snugly without compression. Don't be shy about cramming in fiberglass or mineral wool batts; compression diminishes insulation value. Many inexperienced installers only fill ~75% of the cavity's depth. But even with fluffy R-19 batts, we can fit full coverage in 2x6 framing. Installing insulation, neatly and completely, takes a little finesse.

Here's a step-by-step guide to expert insulation installation:

First, measure the length and depth of each framing bay, to cut batts for custom fit. Use a sharp utility knife to trim batts to size. For angled ceilings or knee walls, contour batts to precisely match the plane. Always cut batts slightly wider than the framing space, so the insulation expands fully.

Next, carefully insert batts between floor joists or wall studs. Gently lift into place rather than forcing or jamming material. Unroll batts to expand insulation and eliminate gaps at seams. Lightly press batts to touch all six sides of the framing cavity.

Where necessary, use insulation-holding nails, along the top of each stud bay. The nails' heads pin up batts neatly and prevent sagging. For vertical applications, like 2x6 plumbing chases, unfaced insulation stays put without any retention. In ceiling applications, install insulation with vapor barrier paper facing down toward the conditioned living space. Usually, rafter baffles provide clearance for ventilated soffit overhangs. Keep insulation from cramming into the baffles, to maintain airflow.

For bonus soundproofing between rooms, glue a second layer of drywall using acoustic sealant before installing insulation. Stagger wall studs for greater sound isolation. Seal all electrical and plumbing penetrations to minimize air leakage and flanking noise transmission.

Insulating rim joists are often overlooked, resulting in crippling heat loss and comfort issues. Use rigid foam cut to fit snugly against foundation sill plates. Adhere foam panels with construction adhesive and secure them mechanically too. Then cover rim joists with continuous batt insulation, doubling up R-values.

Does your floor plan include bonus spaces like dormers or bay windows? Don't neglect insulating these projecting architectural features. Match insulation levels in adjacent walls and ceilings to prevent thermal weak points. Installing insulation properly does take know-how and attention to detail. But, the energy savings and comfort dividends are massive for the small upfront effort. Do it right the first time, and your home will be cozier and more cost-effective for life. New insulation materials emerge constantly as technology evolves. However, the installation techniques remain fundamentally similar. Whether using fluffy fiberglass batts, rigid foam boards or vacuum-sealed panels, completely filling the entire thermal envelope is key. A continuous plane of insulation without gaps minimizes conductive and convective heat transfer. Consistent insulation levels across all surfaces enables steady, even temperatures throughout the home.

Let's bring our insulation discussion full circle to whole house energy efficiency. Insulating the frame is only one piece of the puzzle, alongside air sealing and high performance windows. Together, these strategies minimize air leakage and heat transfer year-round. Air barrier continuity is just as crucial as insulation coverage. Caulk and foam perimeter cracks, before covering with batt insulation. We'll leave open stud bays for plumbing, wiring, and HVAC until those systems are roughed in. Then comes the final insulation and drywall to button up the thermal envelope.

Our insulation work here sets the stage for heating and cooling systems to operate efficiently. Well-insulated framework stabilizes indoor temperatures, allowing HVAC equipment to maintain comfort using minimal energy. Together with weather-tight windows and doors, quality insulation makes any house feel like a peaceful sanctuary.

Are your build site conditions conducive for frame insulation? Dryness is imperative; dampness causes mold, mildew, and material breakdown. Store insulation away from ground moisture until ready to install. Plan your build schedule, so the roof and exterior are totally dried in before insulation commences. Safety should be top priority when handling insulation. Wear long sleeves, gloves, and eye protection to minimize skin irritation and fiber contact. A dust mask prevents inhaling loose fibers from the air. Review all manufacturer safety precautions for the specific products you're installing. Exercise caution while moving through joists in low headroom areas, like attics and crawl spaces.

In this section, we've explored the science of reducing heat flow, compared insulation materials, calculated R-values, and dutifully installed our insulation throughout the entire thermal envelope. Our snugly insulated frame is now ready for drywall installation, to complete the thermal barrier. In the next chapter, we'll transition from framing, to drywall finishing. I can't wait to see these rooms transform from studs and batts into gorgeous finished living spaces!

Now that the primary cavities are neatly insulated between each stud bay and rafter, it's time to focus on sealing potential thermal bridges. Thermal bridges, also called thermal bypasses, are areas where insulation gets interrupted, enabling heat transmission. Common examples include studs in exterior walls, bottom plates, electrical boxes, and plumbing piping. Though small individually, these dozens of thermal bridges add up to significant energy loss, when left unaddressed. Let's start with wall studs. While cavities fill with plush R-13 insulation, the studs themselves create a conductive path slicing right through. Heat travels easily, via conduction, through the solid wood framing. So, how do we break up this thermal bridge? Continuous insulation is the solution.

By adding a layer of rigid foam insulation on the exterior behind your siding, you can wrap the entire wall surface to stop thermal bridges. Use 1–2 inches of EPS, XPS, or polyiso foam to supplement the cavity batts. Uninterrupted foam insulation confronting the elements keeps exterior walls nice and toasty, with no cold studs poking through. For seriously cold climates, increase continuous insulation to 3–4 inches. You'll also find insulating sheathing options, like Thermoply, to accomplish the same thing. Laminated rigid foam boards provide structure and drainage while insulating wall assemblies. Adhere foam directly to exterior walls with construction adhesive for best results. Then install your choice of siding or rainscreen facade overtop.

While continuous insulation addresses heat loss through wall studs, we still need to tackle those bottom plates. Here, the concrete foundation meets the sole plate, creating a problematic thermal bridge. Once again, rigid foam comes to the rescue. Cut long strips of 2 inch EPS foam and install beneath the bottom plate, before erecting walls. The foam isolates the sole plate from the cold concrete below. For insulation beneath slabs on grade, use 2–4 inches of rigid XPS foam with a high compressive strength. The foam sits between the ground and concrete slab, acting like a thermal break. Some builders even include thick foam on foundation walls, placing a fully insulated thermal envelope underground, too. Add waterproofing membranes below slab foam, to prevent moisture issues.

Once the walls and floors are super tight, you need to consider ceiling penetrations? Recessed can lights, bathroom fans, and attic access hatches puncture through our carefully installed insulation. Air leaks, here, lead to major heat loss, which shows up on thermal imaging as bright hot spots. Make sure to install airtight, IC-rated recessed fixtures that maintain the thermal boundary. Around access hatches and attic entry points, build a short insulated box to butt up against ceiling drywall. Weatherstrip and insulate the hatch cover, so it creates an airtight seal when closed. Use rigid foam, cut to fit around bathroom fan housings and plumbing vents. With each penetration properly sealed, our ceiling insulation can work at full effectiveness.

Speaking of ceiling penetrations, we can't forget about recessed light fixtures poking holes in those perfectly, fluffed attic insulation batts. Left unattended, these recessed lights become like little chimneys, allowing indoor air up into your insulation. Make sure to seal all lighting fixtures with airtight housings and gaskets, so no moisture or air sneaks through. IC rated airtight cans are essential for maintaining performance.

For bonus protection, build a small enclosure around each recessed light, sealed with drywall and canned spray foam. This creates a continuous thermal and air barrier around fixtures. I also recommend using LED lights, which produce very little heat. Keeping recessed lights cool, reduces heat flow up into the attic. Follow all builder's box installation and clearance requirements for fire safety, as well.

Here's an insider building science tip to ensure optimal insulation performance. Install exterior sheathing, housewrap, and window flashings before adding insulation. Why? This sequences the moisture variable layers toward the outside, enabling diffusion outward and downward. Then, a moisture-resistant class I or II vapor retarder batt, can be installed facing the interior. Placing the vapor retarder on the warm side, prevents condensation within wall cavities. Otherwise, water vapor from interior air could get trapped by the insulation and cause mold, rot, or ice dams. We want insulation encased in a complete drainage plane, able to handle water safely. So, sheath and weather barrier first, vapor retarder second, and insulation batting last.

While we're on the subject of weather barriers, let's address a common area of air leakage - electrical boxes in exterior walls. Outlets and switches get framed right into the insulation plane, so we need to seal them up. Start by applying silicone or putty pads around the interior outlet box edges as a first line of defense. For exterior walls, add foam gaskets behind switch plate covers, too. To block air infiltration through electrical boxes more fully, apply a bead of minimally expanding canned spray foam around the exterior box perimeter before insulation. This creates a super tight seal, isolating electrical boxes completely. Just don't fill the whole box solid, or you'll never be able to pull wires! A small bead is all it takes to cut off airflow.

Let's keep improving our thermal envelope with a few more advanced techniques. Next area to address: attic hatches. These large horizontal openings into unconditioned attic space, cause substantial heat loss if uninsulated. Begin by weatherstripping and insulating, the hatch cover itself, to R-30. But, we also need to seal and insulate the surrounding attic opening. Build a custom enclosure around the attic access rough framing using 2x6 studs. Insulate the box fully with R-21 batts, then install airtight drywall on the attic-facing side. Only a drywall hole for the actual hatch door remains. For lots of attic access, double up with interior and exterior insulated covers. With a meticulously sealed and insulated attic access, our ceiling plane regains integrity.

Here's an insider tip for basements and crawl spaces. Don't insulate vaulted rafter bays that project into these vented spaces. Why leave rafter tails exposed? Well, the vented area remains pretty close to outdoor ambient temperature and moisture conditions year-round. If we insulated and air sealed these rafter bays, condensation could accumulate. Leaving the ends of roof rafters uninsulated allows pressure equilibrium with the vented space, for moisture control. Finished attics, garage conversions, and basement buildouts all need insulation tailored to the application. For attics, use spray foam on sloped ceiling rafters, plus R-30 batts on knee walls and dormer walls. In basements, look for closed-cell spray foams that resist moisture. For garage conversions, insulation helps muffle noise from the adjacent parking space. Prioritize fire rated materials in garage walls, too.

Have you heard of double-stud walls or staggered stud assemblies? They're a smart way to beef up wall insulation values, using two rows of staggered studs enclosing continuous insulation between. Basically, you build two parallel stud walls, spaced a few inches apart. The double stud structure leaves a cavity to dump loads of extra insulation into. For a net wall thickness under 14 inches, you can achieve R-40+! Green builders seeking ultimate efficiency might incorporate triple pane windows and doors, as well. But even the highest performing windows cause some heat loss compared to insulated walls. So, adding wide window wraps and jamb extensions maintains the insulation plane around openings. Extend exterior wall insulation a foot or two on either side of windows without blocking the view. High-tech windows and low tech insulation solutions combined achieve optimal thermal performance.

Here's an insider PNW weatherproofing tip. Up in rainy Seattle, we often add rainscreen siding over exterior insulation, to protect building envelopes. An air gap behind the siding allows any moisture to drain down and dry quickly. Otherwise, saturated insulation would cause major mold and rot. Always keep insulation layers safely above drainage planes and protected from precipitation. For green builders, upcycled denim insulation offers an eco-friendly fiber insulation material. Made from 85% recycled denim jeans, this batt insulation boasts nearly the same R-value as fiberglass. The cotton insulation contains zero VOC binders or formaldehyde, too. For sustainable wall and ceiling insulation with character, consider insulating with old blue jeans! The recycled content and natural fiber composition complement eco-friendly builds.

Proper insulation and air sealing work together for optimal efficiency. Before we cover up the framing, take time to seal every crack and gap in the thermal envelope. Caulk warped subfloor seams, spray foam sill plate penetrations, and plug any holes around pipes or wires. Stop air leakage before it even reaches the insulation layer. Why insulate just to let conditioned air sneak out through cracks? Detail work now prevents energy loss for the life of the home.

That covers just about every nook and cranny related to insulating framed walls and attics! Our snugly insulated and air-sealed framework is ready for drywall installation. Let's move ahead in the book to Chapter 9 where we'll transform these insulated cavities into gorgeous finished living spaces. I can't wait to see it come together!

Chapter 9

Installing Drywall on Walls and Ceilings

Grab your drywall saw and utility knife, folks - it's time to start finishing those interior walls and ceilings! Now that the framing is complete, we can enclose the house by fastening drywall panels over the wooden studs and joists. Drywall installation takes time and attention to detail, but it's a crucial step in transforming the structural bones into finished living spaces. Let's dive in! I like to think of drywall sheets as a blank canvas. That glossy white surface holds endless potential for you to turn basic boxes into beautiful rooms. But before we can start decorating and molding our interior design dreams, we've got to hang the drywall properly. A smooth, seamless application requires careful measuring and cutting to size, fastening at regular intervals, and meticulous finishing work.

Don't let those massive 4x8 sheets intimidate you! They're light and easy to handle with a helper or drywall lift. We'll start by going over the essential gear for a safe, efficient drywall job. Safety goggles and a dust mask are a must, along with a retractable utility knife with extra blades. You'll need a T-square for marking neat cuts, along with a straightedge guide for your razor-sharp drywall saw. Don't forget the joint compound, drywall screws or nails, and sandpaper to finish it off. Now let's talk logistics. You'll want to lay sheets out flat, avoiding butt joints right at doorways. Stagger vertical seams, so they don't line up across studs. Plan your layout so scraps are minimized. Measure twice and cut once for each piece, leaving a 1/4 inch gap along floors and ceilings. Dry-fitting sheets, before fastening, allows for the perfect fit.

Here's a pro tip: use dyed screws or nails to create a polka dot pattern, ensuring proper spacing as you secure the board. Fasteners should be at least 1 1/2 inches long, penetrating into the studs every 8 to 12 inches, around the edges, and every 12 to 16 inches across the field.

Sink fastener heads, just below the surface, without ripping the paper. Got an outlet to cut around? Use a RotoZip tool for quick, clean circular cutouts. Make relief cuts from corners when cutting electrical boxes and other openings. Go slowly to avoid cracks at inner corners - we don't want extra joints to finish! For tricky angles, trace the shape onto drywall and follow with your saw. Small gaps can be filled later with a joint compound. Now comes the fun part: spreading creamy joint compound over joints and screw indentations in thin, smooth coats. This is a meditative process that transforms fragmented boards into one continuous surface. Build up layers gradually, allowing sufficient drying time between coats. Feather out edges, so each application blends seamlessly into the last.

Once the compound is dry, it's time to start sanding. Work systematically, from one side of the room to the other, to avoid uneven spots. Apply light, even pressure with the sanding block to smooth away high points and ridges. Be diligent about knocking down edges along seams, as well as inside and outside corners. Thorough sanding now, prevents seeing unsightly lines under the new paint. After that, ceilings come next. Get a helper to hold sheets overhead, as you fasten from below. Start by securing the center row, then work toward walls on either side. Stagger vertical seams between rows and space screws every 7 inches along joists, to prevent sagging. Watch for telltale cracks radiating from corners - a sign of nail pops from truss uplift.

For arched ceilings, secure flexible drywall to curved wooden bracing installed behind. Consider decorative ceiling medallions to cover challenging multi-angle joints. We'll also need to cut holes for can lights and bath fans - be sure to measure precisely, so fixtures overlap edges evenly. Maintaining clean lines, where walls meet sloped, or vaulted ceilings, takes extra care when cutting and sanding for a seamless transition.

Let's circle back to finishing corner beads, which protect vulnerable drywall edges. Use paper-faced metal beads, nailed at stud centers, for durable straight lines on exterior corners. Flexible, vinyl beads create smooth curves along rounded corners. Where walls meet, neat triangular edge trim conceals joints. Apply joint compound over beads, just like regular seams, for a pro-quality look.

While our finishing compound dries, we can turn our attention to the garage. This area tends to get more wear and tear, so moisture-resistant drywall is ideal for preventing damage. Greenboard has a water-repellent core encased in green paper, or use purple board with mold-fighting properties. Be sure to prime and paint garages for maximum longevity. Now, I know you can't wait to personalize your spaces with color and texture. But good drywall finishing is the blank slate that quality decorating relies on. Don't cut corners here - properly installed drywall will stand the test of time. Sand until smooth as silk, double-check for flatness, and take time to fill every last pinhole indentation. Meticulous joint compound application prevents cracks from reappearing later.

Just like with framing, safety and structural integrity have to come before aesthetics when hanging drywall. Prioritizing durable fastening over perfectly aligned seams, prevents major issues down the road. Consistent spacing, with aligned vertical joints, guarantees sturdy anchoring to studs. Rushing leads to sloppy work, being vulnerable to cracking and sagging under pressure.

We've covered a lot of important drywall techniques in this chapter, so let's recap the key steps to keep in mind. First, carefully plan your drywall sheet layout to minimize wasted scraps and unnecessary joints. Use essential tools like a T-square, utility knife, and drywall saw to make clean, precise cuts. Remember to fasten sheets at regular intervals, into the wall studs, with either screws or nails for sturdy attachment. Once sheets are hung, spread the joint compound smoothly over all seams, corners, and screw indentations. Allow the compound to fully dry before sanding down high spots and ridges until the surface is perfectly smooth and seamless. Reinforce exposed corner edges with corner beads for added durability. Finally, work systematically from one side of the room to the other to achieve a flat, consistent finish across the entire surface. Taking the time to follow these vital steps will ensure your drywall looks professionally installed and withstands everyday wear and tear.

I know it seems daunting when faced with a whole house of drywall to hang. But take it room by room, surface by surface, staying focused on quality over speed. Before you know it, those bare wood frames will be transformed into well-insulated, attractive living spaces. With the drywall up, it's amazing how the house suddenly feels like home. Walls that muffle sound make conversations more intimate, while retaining heat keeps rooms cozy and comfortable. We're so close now to adding color, trim, and furnishings to make this place our own. But, not just yet - first we need to complete the drywall finishing process by hanging interior doors neatly into place. They'll transform open doorways into private, peaceful rooms for rest and relaxation. Coming up next, we'll tackle door installation and decorative trim work, to put the final perfect touch on our newly drywalled spaces.

With each carefully fastened drywall sheet, we're not just building a house - we're crafting a nurturing haven for a family's love to blossom within. That makes all the dusty sanding and sore wrists more than worthwhile. Just imagine the joyful voices these rooms will soon echo with, thanks to our diligent efforts today.

Let's discover some more advanced finishing techniques to take your skills to the next level. We'll build on our smooth surface painting prep to create distinctive textures, curves, and accents. Get ready to impress guests with unique designing flair using creative drywall tools and treatments. One easy way to add visual interest is by embossing decorative patterns, right into the wet finishing compound. Press rigid objects like rope, lace, or wire mesh into the mud to leave behind an indented design. Get creative with leaves, ferns, or any textured material. Let the mud fully dry before a gentle sanding to remove edges.

For a more pronounced 3D look, adhere foam medallions, flexible molding strips, or wooden appliques onto drywall before applying joint compound over the entire area. Use putty knives and trowels to create depth and contouring around these dimensional pieces. Experiment with geometric shapes, vines, family crests - the possibilities are endless! Don't be afraid to add freehand textures, either. Practice swirling trowels and stippling brushes to develop your own signature style. Layer on varying thicknesses of mud for multidimensional effects. Add whimsical shapes or animal prints using thumbs and fingers too. Get the whole family involved in crafting a personalized drywall art piece! Looking to add rustic appeal? Try tackling a faux stone or brick treatment. Use painters tape to block off "bricks", then trowel on joint compound in layers to build out each dimensional block. Remove the tape once dry, then use a damp sponge to stipple color variations with mineral pigments. We can also try wood graining by imprinting actual boards into mud before painting. For contemporary spaces, a sleek Venetian, plaster finish adds subtle polish to walls and ceilings. Apply thin coats of lime-based plaster by trowel, allowing to dry fully between layers. Then, use circular motions to burnish the surface smooth with a steel knife or spatula. This creates a luxurious matte sheen full of old world charm.

Beyond flat walls and ceilings, drywall also allows us to build up custom curved and arched elements. Wet mud remains flexible, so we can fasten sheets over solid backing to create rounded contours as a base. Layer joint compound over beads and seams, then carefully sand the dry surface smooth. No square rooms here - we're making every surface sensuously sleek! Drywall arches require extra framing reinforcements to hold their shape without cracking under pressure. Make sure wooden corner bracing, and double top plates are well secured. Use curved drywall sheets designed with tapered edges to follow the arched shape. Fasten screws close together - no more than four inches apart, over the entire surface, to prevent sagging. For a dramatic look, we can use repeating arches to craft tunnel hallways or alcoves. Build temporary curved supports from plywood or 2x4 studs. Cut drywall segments to fit each section, abutting edges tightly before mudding. Slim, rounded doorways also gain distinction framed by an arch header, spanning the opening. Careful measurements ensure a consistent width all the way around.

For more of a grand look, vaulted and tray ceilings add spaciousness and the illusion of height to rooms. Mark stud centers on the floor, first, for easier reference. Support boards with rigid insulation until screws can be driven in. Work systematically from one end, fastening and finishing before moving down the line. For dramatic coffered ceilings, frame down a grid of intersecting beams. This allows recessed panels with molding borders and central medallions. Stagger drywall seams between coffers, to hide long joints. Installing can lights, within each panel, highlights the beautiful contours and dimensions. Just take care ventilating enclosed spaces properly, to prevent moisture buildup.

If you're feeling truly ambitious, we could try our hand at a domed ceiling, inspired by churches or planetariums. Begin by building a curved plywood base, anchored firmly to framing. Use drywall strips, applied vertically with joints staggered, to create a smooth, hemispherical shape. Random orbital sanders help smooth the spherical surface before painting celestial clouds and stars!

With all these options, it may seem overwhelming trying to choose your statement ceiling or accent wall. Remember that drywall allows unlimited chances to reimagine and recreate as your tastes evolve over time. Demoing and replacing drywall is messy, yet straightforward. So, don't stress about committing to just one perfect look! Change your mind in a few years - drywall is the ideal blank canvas awaiting your creativity. The beauty of drywall is in its simplicity and adaptability. With just rectangular sheets, joint compound and paint, we can construct anything from sleek modern planes to old-world textures brimming with character. All those finishing techniques stem from a mastery of drywall fundamentals. Soon you'll have a repertoire of go-to drywall designs, to pull from, for each new project. Dazzle your friends by embossing their family initials above the fireplace. Craft picture frame or chair rail molding from stacked, compound strips. Show off your creative talents decorating kids' rooms with hand-textured animals, frolicking across the walls. Let your imagination run wild!

Chapter 10

Hanging Doors and Installing Trim

The time has come to adorn your framed structure with the finishing details that really make a house a home. Now that the drywall is up on the walls and ceilings, you're ready to install interior doors, hang cabinets, and add moldings and trim throughout the rooms. This final stretch may seem tedious after the heavy lifting of framing, but attention to detail on the trim and fixtures is what separates an amateur project from a professional masterpiece. In this chapter, we'll focus first on selecting and hanging interior doors with an architect's eye for aesthetics. Nothing defines the flow and feeling of a home better than the perfect door, thoughtfully placed to transition between spaces. We'll cover measuring for door openings, choosing door styles and hardware, cutting trim, shimming hinges, and troubleshooting common door hanging problems. With guidance, you'll learn to hang doors with precision to gently glide open while forming an airtight seal when closed.

Beyond the door itself, attractive trim completes the package by flawlessly integrating each door's lines and edges into the surrounding walls. You'll gain essential skills for cutting and fastening multi-piece door casings and laying out elegant crown molding. As we add the exquisite final flourishes, I'll share insider carpenter tricks for efficiently installing trim without sacrificing quality. Soon, you'll stand back to admire doorways with beautifully mitered corners and silhouette lines, gracefully flowing from floor to ceiling.

When it comes to selecting interior doors, you have an inspiring array of options beyond plain old slab and hollow cores. Let your personal style shine through choices, like arched doors lending Old World charm, oversized pocket doors opening up small spaces, or sleek modern doors with bold, horizontally-grained textured wood. Glass panel doors flood adjoining rooms with light, while soundproof doors allow privacy when it's needed most. Don't limit yourself - mix and match door styles throughout the rooms tailored exactly how you please. Pay close attention to the room's purpose when selecting each door. For example, an elegant stained mahogany door adds gravitas to a home office, while whimsical painted French doors keep a playroom light and fun. Make every door selection intentional, and you'll be amazed how new entries and passageways transform the entire home's energy.

When choosing materials, balance your budget with aspirations for beauty and durability. Solid wood doors, like oak, cherry, or mahogany, will stand the test of time with proper care, but don't rule out more affordable, stable engineered doors. For baths and laundry rooms, moisture-resistant doors prevent swelling and sticking. Consider your decorating style too - will painted or stained doors complement the room better? Distressed wood adds cottage charm, while sleek lacquered finishes evoke contemporary cool. Beyond the door itself, selecting compatible knobs, hinges and hardware completes the aesthetic vision. Satin, nickel finishes add an elegant touch to traditional homes, while matte black hardware makes a bold modern statement. Hinge design affects how the door operates - do you prefer self-closing functionality or invisible hinges for a clean, floating look? Make sure knobs and levers have a comfortable shape and scale. The hardware's lasting impression will far outlive any fleeting trends, so choose wisely!

Now that you've envisioned the perfect doors for your home, it's time to make those dreams a reality. Let's get ready to do this proper, with professional techniques for every step. You'll learn all the steps through measuring, cutting, fitting, hanging, and sealing each door for flawless functionality and curb appeal. The vital first step is taking precise measurements of the framed rough doorway opening. Have your tape measure handy to check the height from the floor to the header and the horizontal width at the widest point. Record these measurements to one-sixteenth of an inch - every fraction counts to achieve a gap-free custom fit. If the opening falls between standard door sizes, size down for a snug fit. A tight gap of one-eighth inch all around is ideal.

Next, take the door itself into account. Is it a pre-hung door already outfitted with hinges and jambs or a simple slab only? For pre-hung, confirm it is slightly smaller than the rough opening so it can slip in easily. With slabs, account for adding door jambs and clearance for swinging open without rubbing. Consider which direction the door will swing as you take measurements.

With numbers noted, it's time to transport our doors safely to the worksite. A few strategic precautions will prevent dings and damage en route. Lay the door flat across a padded surface, in a pickup truck bed, or pile the seats high with blankets in a roomy sedan. For pre-hung doors, rest the jamb down, to avoid putting weight on the delicate hinges. Drive slowly and smoothly, avoiding sudden bumps. Upon arrival, keep doors supported on padded sawhorses until installation time. Leaning them risks warping the shape. Acclimate the doors to indoor conditions for a few days, since changes in temperature or humidity can shrink or expand the wood. Inspect each door, now, for any defects or damage from the factory or transport. Address needs for sanding, filing, or planing before you hang them, when it's easiest.

Installation day arrives! Make sure you have all the necessary tools and hardware ready, from shims to nails to wood putty. Carefully double-check the rough opening size - measure twice to hang once! If needed, expand the opening by shaving down stud edges with a handsaw or planer. For pre-hung doors, clear debris and ensure the floor is smooth and level. Have a helper on hand to assist with holding and adjusting the weighty door.

It's finally time to hang our first interior door. Let's lift the pre-hung door into the opening gently, tilting the top in first, at an angle. Adjust and center until there's an even gap on all sides, shimming as needed to make it plumb and level. When positioning is perfect, precisely drive nails through the jambs into the framing studs. Check that it swings freely and seals up tight. Excellent work! For a slab door without pre-attached jambs, we get to customize the fit. Cut boards for jambs to exact height and width, mitering the top corners. Hold the slab in place, centered in the opening temporarily, with nail blocks. Trace the perimeter gap onto the back of jamb boards. Remove and cut along lines with a circular saw to achieve flawless spacing. Reinstall jambs around slab and nail securely into framing.

With the door securely hung, now we integrate it seamlessly into the surrounding space. Carefully measure and cut flat, door casing trim boards, to frame out the jambs and header, mitering the joints for a clean professional appearance. Nail the casing snugly around the door, then caulk cracks. Fill nail holes with wood putty once dry. For a decorative touch, add quarter-round molding where the jamb meets walls.

Beautiful job - now your custom-fit door hangs solidly in place, ready for paint or stain. While it dries, repeat the process to install all your beautifully unique doors throughout the rest of the house. Admire how each door's character informs the feeling of the space it frames. Your home gradually transforms, room by room, as doors define boundaries while simultaneously welcoming flow between them. Let's cover a few other specialized door hanging scenarios as well. Pocket doors require carefully framing the wall to recess the pocket, allowing the door to slide open and disappear totally into the cavity. Make sure to install a sturdy track system, at the right height, for smooth operation. For hinged doors in tight spaces, consider swing-clear, offset hinges, to allow the door to pivot without hitting walls.

Bathrooms often call for sliding barn door hardware, for a space-saving modern twist. Make sure barn door rollers glide silently, along a steel track, secured at the right height. For French doors, with two active doors flanking glass panes, take care to perfectly align both sides and cross-coordinate the hardware finishes for symmetry. No matter the style, every thoughtfully placed door, transforms a house into a welcoming home.

Of course, attaining an architecturally elegant flow between rooms depends on more than the doors alone. Once all doors are hung plumb and true, it's time to complete the picture by installing coordinating trim for flawless finishes. Carefully mitered casing trim, pulls each door into the surrounding space, while crown molding and baseboard tie the walls and ceiling together stylistically. Don't rush the meticulous measuring, cutting, fitting and nailing of trim! This is your chance to add custom finesse with delicate, yet durable, architectural accents. Take time to appreciate the transforming effect of each length of baseboard, crown molding, chair rail, or custom built-in shelving you install. Trim hides flaws while literally elevating rough construction to a finished home. When designing your trim profiles, balance aesthetics with functions, like protecting walls from chair scrapes or anchoring cabinets evenly to walls. Traditional baseboard styles, like simple square, graceful ogee, or carved ranch, add proportional elegance along floor edges.

Crown moldings define where walls meet the ceiling visually; it's so helpful for uneven joints. Built-up or stacked trim adds extra depth, while backband outlines windows gracefully. Don't overlook utilitarian trim like a chair rail with specialized, impact-absorbing profiles. Picture rails make great anchors for hanging artwork while offering protection from nail holes below. For a luxurious touch, add shadow box trim, framing out elegant, coffered ceilings. Apply trim generously, though take care at door headers to leave clearance for swinging open without obstruction. Your thoughtful trim details will delight guests and homeowners alike, for decades to come!

With trim boards selected and designs visualized, it's go time! Let's transform basic framing into exquisitely finished rooms by measuring, cutting, and fastening trim until every last line sings in harmonious proportion. You'll learn efficient techniques, so projects proceed swiftly, while still savoring the satisfaction of precision. Let's trim it out!

First step is gathering materials - stock up on trim boards now to avoid shortages later. For paint-grade trim, versatile primed, finger-jointed pine boards resist warping. More expensive clear solid wood trim, adds a touch of luxury if staining - oak and poplar also take color well. Purchase extras since intricate angled cuts lead to waste. Pre-priming and sanding trim helps speed installation. Have sharp pencils, levels, laser guides and tape measures primed to produce the precise cuts that make everything align. Mark trim lengths directly on boards for efficiency. For flawless miters, carefully transfer angled, corner measurements. A few simple aids, like miter boxes, improve precision.

Next on the list is transforming the rough lumber into gorgeously, grained trim boards ready for installation. Start by cutting boards to overall length with a power miter saw. Its sliding arm allows angled precision better than a hand saw. Make finished cuts just slightly long, for final tweaking onsite. Then adjust the miter saw blade angle to cut exact end miters - double check measurements first! For smaller trim pieces, like quarter round or door casings, a motorized miter box saw quickly makes accurate, angled cuts. Use stop blocks to cut multiple boards all the same length efficiently. No power tools? Carefully hand cut miter joints with backsaws using guides and miter boxes. It just takes more practice to master the technique. A little extra care makes the joints precise.

Pre-assemble trim pieces for each run using finishing nails. This helps visualize proportions and identify any tricky joints that need work, before going on the walls permanently. Use wood putty in seams for smoothness, and then sand and prime all visible surfaces for a flawless, painted finish. Carefully label each pre-assembled section by location - that hard work will pay off during hectic installation. Carefully measure and mark locations, one room at a time. Have an assistant hold lengths in place, for on-the-fly test fitting and adjustments. When positioned perfectly, attach trim to walls and studs with finishing nails.

Work methodically around each room, frequently stepping back to ensure trim lines flow visually. Fill nail holes with putty once secured. Touch up miters or gaps with wood filler, where needed, for seamless transitions. Install crown molding after floors and cabinets are in, to ensure proper fit. Your steady focus and care will result in executed trim details that far surpass expectations. There will inevitably be some trial and error throughout the process - woodworking is hardly ever perfect on the first attempt. But, with patience and practice, each cut and joint improves until mitered corners fit seamlessly and proportions make architectural sense. Stay flexible and keep trying new techniques until they feel mastered. You've got this!

After weeks of meticulous cutting and fitting, the moment of truth arrives. Step back and soak in the completely transformed look and feel of your rooms, now gracefully adorned with elegant trim work. Your steadfast dedication to detail has paid off in the satisfying way each molding and casing integrates, fluidly, into the home's lines. Excellent craftsmanship!

The enriching journey of trim carpentry mastery needn't end here. Continue challenging yourself with more advanced molding styles, stacked layers, built-in shelving, or creative medallions and wall accents. Attend woodworking classes if they inspire you - always keep raising the bar for precision and beauty in your finished trim work. Stay curious and don't stop refining your techniques. We've covered a lot of ground here together! From conceptualizing door designs, to carefully crafting trim profiles, you now have all the skills to adorn your framed interior spaces with functional finishing touches. Elegantly hung doors make way for graceful human movement and connection. Meticulously cut trim pulls it all together stylistically. When doors open and close smoothly, hardware clicks crisply, and trim flows in balanced proportion, you'll know your attention to fine details has paid off.

What's next for our ambitious building project? It's time to outfit the framing skeleton with operational systems to make the house truly livable for happy inhabitants. The upcoming chapter will guide you through planning and integrating essential plumbing, HVAC, and electrical systems into the home's infrastructure. With wiring and ductwork threaded through the framing, plus appliances and fixtures connected just where needed, we'll progress from an empty shell to a warm, powered-up dream home.

Onward we go to the next chapter!

Chapter 11

Finishing Touches - Railings, Cabinets, and Closets

By the time you get to the finishing stages of your framing project, you'll be eager to see all your hard work come together into a beautiful, livable space. Well, my friend, we're almost there! But first, we need to add those special touches that really make a house a home. In this chapter, I'll walk you through creating the kind of elegance and refinement that impresses guests and delights you every time you walk through your custom-crafted doorways.

Beyond the standard doors and trim, we'll dive into crafting built-ins and storage solutions that maximize your living space. I'll share framing techniques for gracefully integrating shelving, cabinetry, benches and media centers into your floor plan. A well-designed reading nook under the stairs can transform wasted space into a cozy escape. Picture a lovely window seat flanked by bookshelves - doesn't that sound like the perfect reading spot on a rainy day?

We'll build custom closets and drawers tailored to your unique needs, so everything has a place. An elegant coat rack or mirror by the entryway makes a grand first impression. Ever dreamed of a window bar where you can mix cocktails while gazing at the sunset? With some creative framing, you can build the wine cellar or dry bar of your dreams! For a chef's kitchen, let's design a spacious island complete with storage for pots and pans right within reach. Add a frame-mounted drying rack and custom spice shelves on the walls. With some open shelving made from reclaimed wood, your kitchen will feel cozy and lived-in, but still sleek. For the butler's pantry, we can frame glass-front cabinets to showcase all your fine china and linens.

In the bathroom, think about luxurious built-in bathtub platforms with steps and storage beneath. We can frame a standing sink vanity with tall linen cabinets on each side. Add some recessed niches in the shower to stash shampoos in style. The possibilities for custom woodwork are endless - whatever your vision, we can build it! Now, if you really want to elevate the charm factor, let's install some detailed casings around each window and doorway. Picture ornate pediments accenting the tops of windows or doors for a graceful decorative touch, straight out of Versaille. For a Mediterranean villa vibe, we could add some hand-carved wood corbels supporting a timber mantle beam.

If your tastes run more modern, clean-lined frames and floating shelves have an elegant simplicity. We can construct long built-in banquettes, flanked by expansive windows, to unite indoor and outdoor spaces. Minimalist designs feel serene and timeless when executed with quality materials and precision craftsmanship. As we add paneling, wainscoting, and other decorative woodwork, notice how each piece enhances and complements your home's architecture. Trim framing is about unity, bringing all the structural components together into a harmonious living space. It takes an artistic eye and a steady hand to miter precise seams and align trim just so. But with care and patience, you'll create lasting beauty worth framing and hanging on the wall!

Now for the fun part: choosing gorgeous hardware like doorknobs, handles, hooks and knockers to adorn your doors and cabinets. A unique front door handle makes a great first impression, while backplates and knobs throughout your home express personal style. Sleek levers and black wrought iron handles lend an air of sophisticated elegance. Pewter or copper knobs and pulls add a rustic, timeworn feel.

For exterior doors, a handsome knocker or entry set conveys welcome and charm. I recommend sturdy mortise locks instead of flimsy spring latches for better security, too. Add some character to plain doors by framing recessed panels or carving simple designs. Distressed or vivid colors can complement your decor, while natural wood tones match any style. Take time installing each knob and lock, perfectly straight and centered - the small details make all the difference. Step back frequently to see how the trim you're framing enhances the home as a whole. Adjust any corners that aren't completely plumb, and sand imperfections until the surfaces are buttery smooth.

Soon you'll have all your family and friends oohing and aahing over the high-end details that elevate your home. They'll compliment your sophisticated taste as you give a tour of the finished spaces. You'll take pride in pointing out the quality construction and custom touches you added throughout. Then you'll smile, thinking back on all the hours you invested to create such beauty.

While you have the saws out, let's add some personalized touches like picture frames, message boards, and name signs on bedroom doors. For a rustic cabin, we could frame some hand-painted signs or antlers as wall art. Show off your hobbies and interests through custom woodwork - shelves to display collectibles, a frame for your golf clubs, or racks to hold wine bottles and fishing poles. If you're artistically inclined, this is the perfect time to add decorative woodwork like carved signs, trim accents, murals, or custom mirror frames. Make your kitchen feel lively and lived-in with some framed photos or kids' artwork on the fridge. Add whimsical carvings along the legs of a bench or bordering window panes. The options for personalization are endless - have fun and make your home distinctly yours!

For a final crowning touch, let's craft custom cornices and valances to adorn your windows. We'll construct graceful curves or angular facades to suit your decor. Picture luxurious swagged drapes atop arched transoms and elongated windows for a dramatic designer look. With creatively framed windows as the focal point, your rooms will feel bathed in natural light and elegance.

Now that we've finished framing the core structure and installing interior doors and trim, it's time to focus on integrating essential systems like plumbing, electrical and HVAC into your custom framework. Beautiful finishes are wonderful, but your home also needs to function efficiently to provide comfort year-round.

In Chapter 12 we'll plan how to run wiring and ductwork through walls, ceilings and floors without compromising structural integrity. I'll share tips for allowing access to mechanical systems for maintenance down the road. We'll choose energy-efficient HVAC components tailored to your climate and construction.

Designing lighting systems and switch circuits is both practical and creative. Picture installing stylish fixtures above your kitchen sink or recessed lights to spotlight art in the living room. We'll add electrical outlets conveniently throughout the home so you can plug in lamps, appliances, and entertainment systems anywhere needed. When it comes to plumbing, we'll strategically place water supply lines and drains. I'll demonstrate insulating pipes properly to prevent freezing or sweating. You'll learn to install elegant faucets, shower heads, and other fixtures in your beautifully tiled bathrooms and laundry room.

With insulation, wiring, and ductwork neatly integrated into your framing, you'll have a comfortable, efficient, and well-functioning home to enjoy for years to come. So get excited as we transition to the next chapter, where we'll build on your beautiful structure by seamlessly incorporating state-of-the-art systems throughout. Well done completing this ambitious chapter! You've leveled up your skills tremendously.

Chapter 12

Planning Plumbing, Electrical, and HVAC

The structural framework is finally built, and it's time to make your house truly livable by planning the systems that allow it to function: plumbing, electrical, and HVAC (heating, ventilation, and air conditioning). Though it may seem daunting to coordinate all these complex networks of pipes, wires, vents, and machinery, this chapter breaks the process down into manageable steps. We'll discuss how to effectively design each system and integrate them within the home's framework. Having clean water flow from every faucet, lights turn on at the flip of a switch, and your climate-controlled perfectly, are essentials that make a house a comfortable home. It's staggering to think about the miles of wiring and plumbing hidden in walls and under floors that make modern living possible! Proper planning is crucial - once the drywall is up, it's far more difficult to change things. So, let's dive in and master the ins and outs of planning your home's nervous system.

We'll start with plumbing, since it directly provides one of life's most vital resources - water. Begin by reviewing your floor plan and making note of all fixtures that require water supply and drainage. Kitchen sinks, bathroom vanities, showers/tubs, laundry hookups, exterior hose bibs for gardening, and icemaker refrigerator lines - account for every water-fed component in the house. Don't forget appliance considerations, like whether you want instant hot water taps or a pot filler faucet in the kitchen.

Next, determine the incoming water supply point, which should connect to your main shutoff valve and pressure regulator. Locate all drain and vent outlet points. Will this tie into an existing sewer system, or will you need a septic tank installed? Draw straight lines connecting fixtures to the water supply and sewer/septic connections to map out the main water and drain lines. This schematic will guide your plumbing layout.

Now consider each fixture's hot and cold water needs. Group bathrooms and kitchens together where possible to consolidate hot water lines. Determine one or multiple water heater locations to efficiently serve all outlets. For a large house, multiple tankless heaters may provide better simultaneous hot water flow. Calculate the BTUs needed to size heaters and use insulated piping to minimize heat loss.

Gravity is our friend for drainage. Slope drain lines at least 1/4 inch per foot downward toward the main sewer/septic connection. Avoid flat horizontal runs where gunk can collect. Vent pipes also require thoughtful layout - they allow air into drain lines to prevent vacuum lock and allow sewer gas to vent outside. Include vent stacks at key junction points and route them up through the roof. With basic supply and drainage schematics mapped out, refine the plan with pipe sizing. Larger main lines branch into smaller fixture feeds - generally 1/2 inch lines suffice for sinks and toilets. Make sure you have 3/4 inch or larger lines for high flow items like washing machines, dishwashers, and showers. Avoid excessive flow restrictions. Include shutoff valves throughout the system for maintenance access.

Choose quiet, corrosion resistant piping, like PEX or PVC. Copper offers durability but noisier flow. Cast iron is still best for main drains. ABS plastic works well for vents. Follow all code requirements and don't cut corners - leaks and clogs equal headaches down the road! Think about water conservation features, like low-flow toilets and faucets, too.

Now let's switch over to the electrical system, which literally powers your home. We'll need to provide adequate power outlets, lighting, safety systems, and wiring capacity for all current and future electrical loads. As with plumbing, start by evaluating your floor plan and creating a master schematic. Map locations for switches, outlets, lighting fixtures, smoke detectors, CO sensors, doorbells, and any special power needs, like a hot tub hookup. Determine the main service panel location and layout major branch circuits from there. Follow the code for required circuit capacity and proximity - having enough amps and outlets avoids nuisance tripping and extension cord spaghetti. Include dedicated 20 amp circuits for high power areas, like kitchens and laundry. Lighting circuits, smoke detector circuits, and outlets can share 15 amp branches. Have at least one GFCI protected circuit per room.

Now, layer in home technology wiring, since this gets embedded in walls too. Will you have whole home audio-visual, surveillance cameras, smart home controls, electric vehicle charging? Pre-wire for any systems, now, even if not installing immediately. It's wise to oversize the conduit and leave pull strings for adding future wiring. You can never have too much capacity! Choose copper or aluminum for most wiring - inexpensive yet durable. Utilize metal clad or flexible conduit between walls and junction boxes for protection. Circuit breaker panels are standard, but for sophisticated whole home control, consider a smart panel. These let you monitor energy use and remotely control circuits from your phone!

Take time to research your lighting design. Fixtures enhance aesthetics while providing essential illumination. For general ambient light, use energy-saving LED bulbs in recessed can lights. Accent lighting, like track lights, highlights artwork or architectural details. Under and over cabinet lighting creates useful task lighting in kitchens. Outdoor lighting extends living space into the landscape for nighttime enjoyment while improving safety and security monitoring.

Now let's tackle the HVAC systems that heat and cool your home. A well-designed system keeps you comfortable year-round while maintaining healthy indoor air quality and humidity levels. We need equipment properly sized for the house, and smart ductwork layout to evenly distribute conditioned air. Zoning allows custom heating and cooling control in different areas.

Start by determining the heating and cooling load - the BTUs of energy needed to maintain desired temperatures. Factor in insulation values, home orientation, window area, and local climate stats. Oversizing equipment reduces efficiency, while undersizing can't keep up on extreme days. Heat pump systems provide both heating and AC from a single outdoor unit, saving cost and space. When designing the ductwork, keep optimal airflow in mind. Size main supply and return ducts large, about 18 inches wide, reducing branching runs. Limit bends for smoother air delivery. Take advantage of ceiling height in upper floors to run ducts there. Register vents, placed high on walls, effectively mix air without blasting cold air down on you! Return vent location matters too.outside. Proper ventilation greatly improves indoor air but is often neglected. Incorporate bathroom exhaust fans, kitchen range hoods, laundry room venting, and fresh air intake. Consider a whole house ventilation system, or HRV, to automatically exchange indoor/outdoor air. This removes contaminants, allergens, and musty smells.

Advanced features, like zoned controls, humidifiers, media air filters, and smart thermostats, boost comfort, efficiency, and health. I recommend installing the home run wiring, even if holding off on the control system purchase. Built-in wifi and app connectivity make today's HVACs incredibly responsive without getting up! Comprehensively planning the home's plumbing, electrical, and HVAC gives you immense control over its functionality for years to come. These "boring" backstage systems truly enable comfortable daily living.

Remember to stay engaged with the various contractors to spot any deviations from the master plan, and head off issues immediately. For example, a misplaced drain line must be rerouted before embedding in concrete. Service access and shut-offs should also be convenient, not walled off impractically. Little planning tweaks, now, avoids major headaches down the road.

Though it takes diligence and coordination, the payoff is huge in homeowner enjoyment and peace of mind. There's nothing more frustrating than a clogged pipe you can't unclog, or an electrical panel that lacks capacity for a simple upgrade. Investment in robust infrastructure is like your home's insurance policy. Hopefully, you never need to "file a claim", but boy is it worth it when catastrophe strikes! Throughout construction, safety is also paramount when installing these complex systems. Protect against electrocution, flood damage, HVAC unit tip overs, and more by following best practices and code. Patience and care now prevents pipes from freezing, wires shorting, and other dangerous malfunctions. Your home should sustain and enrich life.

Once all systems are installed and inspected, the final step is learning them intimately yourself, regardless of using professional long term service. Know where valves and switches are. Test them periodically and fix minor issues immediately. Perform preventative maintenance like drain flushing, duct cleaning and replacing worn electrical outlets and corroded pipes before they fail. A clean furnace filter saves many headaches down the road. Consider installing a whole home surge protector and even backup generator if your region has frequent outages. Weather-related power events are increasing, so better safe than a freezer full of spoiled food! For plumbed appliances, like refrigerators and washing machines, ensure hoses have auto shut-off valves in case of hose rupture. Take time to prep your home's systems for resilience against the unexpected.

Whether you're embarking on new construction or upgrading existing home systems, Hopefully, this chapter provides a comprehensive overview of the planning process. We covered a ton of ground, but breaking it down step-by-step demystifies the infrastructure fundamentals needed in any high-functioning home. It may seem like a lot of effort up front, but the dividends over your home's lifetime are invaluable. Once these "boring" backbones of plumbing, HVAC and electrical are fully planned, it's exciting to switch gears to the finishing details of bringing your home to life. Creating character through interior finishes and smart storage is the fun creative work that personalizes a space. Lighting and landscaping add ambiance by night.

Selecting attractive, durable finishes is an exciting part of making a house your home. While we've thoroughly planned the core infrastructure, don't underestimate how much small aesthetic choices impact the living experience.. Clever storage solutions remove clutter to create calming spaces. Quality flooring holds up to busy family life. Choosing flooring, a complex choice balancing durability, easy maintenance, comfort underfoot, and visual appeal. Budget dictates options, but well-installed floors endure decades of heavy traffic. Consider your lifestyle as you evaluate materials room by room. For example, moisture-resistant ceramic tile, works well in baths and laundry rooms, while plush carpet creates a cozy bedroom retreat.

Tile and stone offer unmatched durability, with quality installation being key. Check subfloor preparation and use proper setting materials to avoid cracked grout or tiles lifting over time. Slate and Saltillo tiles add rustic Old World charm. Polished marble and granite exude elegance, and mosaics create artistic flair, especially in accent walls or backsplashes. Engineered wood floors impress with textural grain patterns reminiscent of hardwood, but with added stability and moisture resistance. Brands, like Shaw and Mannington, mimic everything from weathered barnwood planks to exotic tropical hardwoods. Factory finishes reduce site work and VOCs.

Carpet remains are popular for insulating noise and providing soft comfort underfoot. Today's styles range from practical stain-resistant saxonies and textured friezes, to lush plushes exceeding 5000 grams dense fiber weight. Use quality cushion padding to double carpet's life expectancy. Regular professional steam cleaning restores appearance and sanitizes.

Beyond flooring, unique lighting transforms sterile spaces into inviting, artistic ambiances. Thoughtful fixture layout flatters everyone by casting light from multiple angles to reduce shadows. Dimmer switches enable modifying mood and brightness. For kitchen task lighting, LED under-cabinet lights illuminate countertops without glare, and rope lights lining stairs aid visibility while adding flair.

In baths, moisture resistant, recessed can lights supplement vanities, while skylights introduce natural light. Outdoor lighting extends living space into the landscape and improves home security. Uplighting or downlighting architectural elements creates dramatic evening shadow effects.

Now let's explore how clever storage solutions can make a home feel larger by keeping clutter contained neatly out of sight. Built-in cabinetry maximizes unused nooks and crannies with customized shelving. Basement storage systems keep seasonal items accessible but tidy, and closet organization products multiply hanging capacity.
Consider your unique needs room by room. In entryways, wall hooks or benches stash shoes/bags out of the traffic path. The kitchen island could benefit from rollout trays or drawer dividers for cooking gadgets. Add pull-out spice racks and pantry shelving for food items. Enhance laundry efficiency with hanging rods, hampers and fold-out ironing boards.

Bedrooms need nightstands with charging docks and hidden storage. Expand closet space with double hanging rods and stacked shelving reaching to the ceiling. Get creative with space under beds - it's prime real estate for plastic underbed bins holding clothing, linens and memory books. The garage, especially, tends to become a disorganized mess; incorporate wall cabinets, pegboards and overhead storage to cleanly store tools and sporting equipment.

Beyond interior touches, exterior finishes and landscaping make a great first impression, adding character that reflects your personal style. A fresh coat of exterior paint works wonders, choosing dynamic accent colors to make architectural details pop. Include artistic touches, like stenciled designs, faux brickwork, or hand painted quotes.

Front door flair shows off your personality with unconventional colors like emerald green, bright red, or turquoise. Give worn, fiberglass entry doors new life with distressed plank wood refacing kits. Upcycle large old windows into custom picture frame breezeway doors. Even adding striking new house numbers or a giant blooming flower pot, makes a statement. Yard and garden landscaping instantly boosts curb appeal. Sculpt greenery into living works of art through strategic plant placement, rows of uniform shrubs, or topiaries adorning the mailbox. Install hardscaping, like stacked stone planter walls and brick paver walkways. Finally, ensure adequate exterior lighting to both guide visitors and elegantly accent architectural features by night.

This chapter aimed to spark creative ideas for incorporating charm through lighting, storage, floors, trims and more. Take inspiration from your favorite public buildings and parks, travel memories, even snippets in home magazines you admire. Include special touches honoring your family heritage or interests, like nautical themes near water or pottery accents from your artistic grandmother. Finishing is also a wonderful opportunity to support local artisans, shops, and contractors passionate about their craft. Handcrafted tile, custom-built cabinetry, and forged ironwork infuse homes with quality, durability, and character mass-produced items often lack. Take pride in the artistry you're supporting. Surround yourself with finishes and decor that bring joy, aid living and connect with your priorities. Perfectly appointed interiors matter little if clutter and chaos still reign. If your tastes evolve, freedom comes from knowing finishes can be refreshed, replaced, or painted over in the future as needs change. Your home should empower both function and flexibility.

With a well-planned foundation, weather-tight enclosure, and functioning infrastructure complete, we're ready for the fun part -personalizing the home with creative finishing touches! But, even amidst the flurry of final decor decisions, remember to pause and be profoundly grateful for having a place to call your own. May your home overflow with joy shared with others. On that heartfelt note, we near the end of our home building journey together. What an incredible learning experience it has been! In our final chapter, we'll recap key lessons from foundation to finish. I'll share wisdom and warnings so you can maintain your home for health, efficiency, and happiness long term. When one chapter of repairs or upgrades ends, a new one inevitably waits around the corner. Homeownership is a perpetual adventure!

Printed in the USA
CPSIA information can be obtained
at www.ICGtesting.com
LVHW012143090324
773914LV00012B/695